TEACH US HOW TO PRAY

TEACH US HOW TO PRAY

LOUIS EVELY *translated by Edmond Bonin*

PAULIST PRESS

Paramus, N.J.   New York, N.Y.

This book is a translation of Apprenez-nous à prier *and* Sur la prière.

Nihil obstat: Rev. Donald J. Gervais, *Censor Deputatus*

Imprimatur: ✠ Bernard J. Flanagan, *Bishop of Worcester*

April 21, 1967

ISBN 0-8091-1780-0

Library of Congress Catalog Card Number: 67-26074

Published by Paulist Press

Editorial Office: 1865 Broadway, N.Y., N.Y. 10023

Business Office: Paramus, N. J. 07652

Printed and bound in the United States of America

Contents

Prayer

We don't know how to pray any more. Prayer is a lost art, with very few teachers or schools left. Do you know of any churches where, on Sunday, we learn how to pray, where we actually do pray and are lifted up on a wave of prayer? They're few and far between.

We pray so little, so rarely and so poorly. Though we feel bad about it, we don't see what we could possibly do. First of all, we're very busy people; our life is so crammed with activities, distractions and sometimes even good works, that there's always too much going on and we don't have a minute for anything else. As a result, we're swayed by our weakness, cowardice and whims. Since we always have a thousand enterprises to choose from, we always find pretexts—good ones, pious and charitable ones—to avoid what we don't feel like doing, what we dread doing: that is, stopping, concentrating, and praying. We'd rather do anything but occupy ourselves with God. This solemn confrontation alarms us, for we're afraid to be bored, to learn what we don't care to know, and be talked into sacrificing what we don't wish to surrender.

Above all, we don't have time for God. Deep down, we're convinced we'd be wasting it on him; and goodness knows we can't afford that with so many matters craving our attention. If God is almighty, our negotiations with him ought to move faster, we should be able to reach a quick understanding and be through.

1

His slowness in revealing himself, acting and explaining his ways annoys us. For everything else, however, we have plenty of leisure. Visits, get-togethers, movies, football games, concerts, an evening with friends, an invitation we can't decline—too bad, but we simply have to fit all this in, for it's only right and natural that these people make demands on us and our time. But when God lays claim to our time, we balk; that's too much, it's intolerable, and no modern man or woman can put up with it. Imagine his begging for some of our precious time! We'll give him our works, our name, our voice and even our money if we must, but he'd better not ask for time. After all, when dealing with God, why need we rattle on and beat around the bush? Accordingly, we enter, summon him and lay our cards on the table. Then, without listening to his reply, we leave. What shocking neglect shows through this impatience, this arrogant haste! "But I'm in a rush," we explain, "I'm pressed for time."

Actually, it's a vicious circle: we're so weak (precisely because we don't pray) that we approach all our problems from a tangent, forever procrastinating in the hope that the longer we wait, the stronger we'll be to tackle them. So we dawdle for weeks and months without writing that certain letter or taking that necessary step or making that vital decision. The less we work, the more we're burdened by the tasks we've left undone and the many obligations we can't meet. Then, when someone comes along and suggests we should pray over and above that, we rebel and lash out frantically as if he were trying to strangle us. Still, if we were heroic enough to start by praying for an hour at

the beginning of a hectic day, we might be so strengthened and so well nourished that we'd no longer fear
anything, but rather meet every danger, every sacrifice
and every suffering head-on, and, amazed at having
finished so early, find yet more time to pray at night.

Even those of us who hunger for God, those who
want to pray, literally starve to death near the banquet
table because we lack the courage to sit down and eat.
Just as the harried housewife can't stop running to and
fro, waiting on everyone, urging them to eat and lung-
ing for dishes and spoons till she herself becomes so
keyed-up that she's no longer hungry and can't swallow, so the best among us discourse on the need and ef-
ficacy of prayer and invite others to try it but are ultimately too tense and exhausted to do so ourselves.

God wants quiet; he works in silence; he needs
serenity to act, and time to calm us down. Like present-
day servants, he insists on one point: that we treat him
with consideration, that we take time and trouble to
think of him. God acts and works only with time. In
prayer, he's not the one who must change (otherwise,
prayer would surely be instantaneous); we're the ones
who must gradually be changed—we and our slowness,
our hesitation, our attachment to the very evil we hope
to be delivered from, and our dread of the grace we
think we're imploring. We come before him wholly
taken up with ourselves, obstinate in our desires, and
half-crazed with the complaints of our flesh and the
clamor of our appetites. As a Trappist friend of mine
once said, "There's no slamming on the brakes and
stopping our car on a dime if the motor inside keeps

whirling at top speed." We can plop our body on a chair, but our anxious, indocile, ravening mind continues to fret and agitate itself futilely within us. It takes time—a long time—for the engine to decelerate and for us to move in rhythm with God; to adjust our tempo to his tempo, our will to his will, and our steps to his steps; to enter into a state of relaxation and recipience; and to subdue our interior pulsations so that we may begin to share in his peace. Modern physicists attribute the resistance of bodies to the rapidity of molecular vibrations. From our own experience, we know that a nervous stomach can't assimilate food, and, on another level, that trepidation blocks receptivity. We often complain that we don't know God because he's silent, remote, absent; but God doesn't fail us: it's we who fail him.

Of all beings in heaven and on earth, God is the most alive and active. "My Father goes on working," said Jesus, "and so do I."[1] That Trappist friend once told me, "I'm like a drinking glass that's too small for the amount of water poured into it. The moment I kneel, the moment I recollect myself, everything spills over." God is preeminently like that: himself a fountain of living water, he has promised that those who drink that water will have "a spring inside them welling up to eternal life."[2] Ours is the religion, not of God's absence, but of his presence—of his real presence despite his invisibility.

[1] Jn. 5, 17. (All scripture quotations are from *The Jerusalem Bible.*)
[2] Jn. 4, 14.

God may be invisible to our eyes, but he becomes visible to the soul that prays. There's nothing more present, more manifest or more operative than God once we open our soul to him. If we want to let him in, be filled with him and start kindling at the touch of his flame, we must be willing to pray for three hours at a stretch. All we have to do is sacrifice to him the time we so gladly devote to a play, a movie, or a baseball game.

One day the apostles followed Jesus to a solitary spot—a craggy, silent mountaintop, far from the crowds where they usually acted important and officious, like influential mediators. There, in that peaceful atmosphere, they gradually composed themselves, started seeing things in perspective and became attentive to Jesus; until, focusing on him alone and open to his influence, they unsealed their eyes and beheld him for a moment as he really was all the time.

Do we honestly want to see Jesus and his glory? Do we want him to manifest himself and be transfigured before us? Then, we should devote a morning to him, or spend an evening in church or a whole afternoon in some beautiful tree-girt meadow with only the Gospels for company. If we do so, we can expect (and if we've already done it, we know) that, bit by bit, in the hush of the chapel or the stillness of nature, our eyes will slowly open and we'll start seeing him and ourselves very clearly. We'll discover what we're now hiding—the evil we do, whether we're conscious of it or refuse to advert to it. We'll hear his voice, those words he's always speaking to us though we try so desperately not to hear. We'll see plainly what he expects of us. His presence will grow so real and immediate that it may oppress us somewhat; his face will become radiant, more magnetic than anything we've ever known. Like so many others before us, we'll exclaim, "Lord, it's good to be with you! If only I could always be like this and never change. . . . Let me pitch my tent here and stay forever."

What Is Prayer?

What do we mean by prayer? What's so great and terrible about it that it scares us to death? Unfortunately, we've forgotten what. We've drifted so far from prayer that by now we're quite convinced it's a purely human activity, a summons, a speech we make to God. No longer do we realize that he's the one who prays in us. Remember Chantecler? Persuaded that it was his crowing which awakened the sun, he felt certain the day could never break without him. But the truth was far more beautiful than he dreamed. With the first pale rays of dawn, it was the sun that awakened Chantecler, and he was only the harbinger of all the warmth and light and goodness at the heart of the universe. We make the very same mistake with regard to prayer and behave as if we'd been deputed to rouse a sleeping God, move an indifferent God, contact a far-away God.

What a sorry picture we paint of him! Unconsciously, we invent a God who resembles us—cold and unfeeling, bored and vaguely dissatisfied. As Voltaire quipped, "God created men in his image and likeness, and in return they've been doing the same to him." Unless we watch out, we fabricate a God so pitiful that we're sure we'd be better than he. For example, almost all of us feel that we would have endowed ourselves more richly than God has, and that we would have been more generous, more beneficent and merciful toward ourselves than he's been. Before every battle, LaHire, the rough-and-ready captain whom Joan of Arc had converted, used to kneel and say a prayer which he had composed in the naiveté of his heart and which at bottom was pure blasphemy: "Lord, do for LaHire what he'd do for you if you were LaHire and he were God." It was tantamount to saying, "Try your best to be as good as I am!" Many of us wouldn't want to be the God we've dreamed up: we'd be far better than that.

But the fact is that God is better than we could ever imagine. He's supremely good. It's he who wants to give, and men who don't want to receive. He has pleaded with mankind, says Pascal, but we haven't listened to him. According to Saint Augustine, God wants to give infinitely more than we want to receive. How encouraging it is to realize suddenly that prayer is supernatural, that it's a gift—something God does in us. When we kneel to pray in church or at home, we should first shout for joy and laugh aloud with sheer delight. For God is at work, he's here toiling in us, he has begun undermining our dogged resistance and has already obtained his first victory from us—the unbelievable fact that we've started to pray. And now, if we persevere, if we wait long enough, we'll learn exactly how he has already heard us.

Our whole religious life is supernatural and, therefore, inspired. Without the stimulus and help of the Holy Spirit, we can't really pray or make a single act of genuine faith, hope, charity or repentance. "The Spirit . . . comes to help us in our weakness. For when we cannot choose words in order to pray properly, the Spirit himself expresses our plea in a way that could never be put into words."[1]

[1] Rom. 8, 26.

Praying means surrendering to the influence of the Holy Spirit, becoming calm and recollected, so that we may grow docile as he prays in us, till our innermost activities ooze out, trickle and finally gush forth under his inspiration.

Praying means making way for someone greater than we, letting the Son's joy and his love for the Father awaken in us and fill us to overflowing. There's only one prayer the Father loves and listens to with unbounded rapture, and that's the ceaseless murmur of love, desire, reverence and admiration which rises to him from the heart of his Son. To be authentic, our every prayer must echo his. Praying, then, means allowing the Spirit—the Son's love for the Father—to spring from our hearts to our lips.

Lastly, praying means placing ourselves at God's disposal so that, for a moment or two, he may accomplish what he has always wanted to do in us and what we never give him a chance to. We're like sullen, obstinate children whose father wants to help them admit their guilt, so he can tell them they're forgiven. Aware of what he's trying to do, they stay on guard, keep to themselves and avoid his presence. When that's impossible, they always manage to have a third person around; and when that doesn't work, they play dumb and pretend they don't understand his peace overtures. Otherwise, you see, it'd be horrible. For they know full well that if they let themselves be influenced, if they stayed with him awhile and listened to him, they'd immediately feel sorry, start crying and beg forgiveness, only to find out that they already had it. In a word, they'd understand that they were brought to ask forgiveness only because he had forgiven them and was dying to tell them so.

That's how God is—just as good. And that's why we habitually keep a safe distance from him, for it's dreadful what he can give us and achieve in us once we allow him to. Nothing transforms us like this kind of prayer; nothing does so much good or inflicts so much pain. It's a continuous activity, almost imperceptible (like the progress of the hour hand around a watch), and yet so powerful it hurts. When we're plugged into God's current, it circulates through our inmost self and we perceive that we're completely changed.

Let me illustrate what I mean. A mother comes to pray because her child is sick and she doesn't want him to die. The doctor just told her, "I've tried absolutely everything. All we can do now is resign ourselves to the inevitable." She neither believed the doctor nor listened to her husband as he tried to reason with her. Instead, she told both of them what she thought: "You're giving up too easily; but I won't abandon my son like you, because I'm sure he can still be saved." So here she is in church. She has come to tell God that her boy mustn't die, that he simply can't, that she doesn't want him to, that God couldn't permit such a thing. Then, by dint of praying—if she does it sincerely and long enough—she enters into a deeper prayer. Slowly, the detachment she ruled out begins to permeate her; and when she gets up, she's amazed to hear herself say, "Lord, I entrust him to you. From this moment on, he's your child much more than mine. I know he's better off in your hands. You're responsible for him now, and you'll take better care of him than I ever could. May your will be done!"

Jesus himself prayed that way. At first he pleaded, "Father, everything is possible for you. Take this cup away from me." Then, because he stayed the whole night through, he entered into a deeper prayer and arose saying, "Let your will be done, not mine."[2]

If we try to pray like that, if we try to submit to this transforming power, we'll feel our earlier attitude change under the spell of prayer. We come weighed down with burdens, crushed under mountains of care, resentment, sadness, obsession and fear. Never could we lift them, never free ourselves. We're everlastingly pinned to the ground. And then, as we pray, God slowly rises up, manifests himself and starts to act. God becomes God before our eyes. Now all the knots slip loose and the mountains float away. Though we can't explain it, they're sailing around us like clouds that we could blow about or brush aside with our little finger. It's true that prayer moves mountains and walks on the sea. When God becomes God in our life, everything changes and yet remains the same: all our questions are answered and all our ills healed solely because God has resumed his rightful place and we've returned to ours. God is God once more; he's good, wise, happy and close to man, and these are all reasons for us to be joyful and confident. As for us—well, we're not important. We've become free again, cheerful and light-

---

[2] Mk. 14, 36 and Lk. 22, 42.

hearted and true. Why be so concerned over problems that affect inconsequential beings like us? Still, insignificant though we are, the Father loves us and always carries us in his arms.

This is the miracle God performs in us. Since he alone can act in the depths of our soul, his works enable us to recognize him unmistakably and place our trust in him. When the Samaritan woman went back to her fellow villagers, she said, "Come and see a man who has told me everything I ever did." They doubtlessly jeered, "Well, that gave him plenty to talk about!" But once they had seen and heard him for themselves, they begged him to stay with them. When he left, two days later, they said to her, "Now we no longer believe because of what you told us; we have heard him ourselves and we know that he really is the saviour of the world."[3]

When we've prayed and been transformed like this, we can tell our priests and retreat masters, "I believe not only because you've taught me about Christ, but because I've heard him for myself and know he can save the world. He has spoken to me personally and transformed me, and I see that he has the power to save me."

[3] Jn. 4, 29. 42.

Praying with Faith

Jesus prayed. He used to retire to secluded spots and pray; and when he came back, quite transparent with fervor and radiant with love and bliss, his disciples envied him and said, "If only we could pray like that! It's too bad we can't. . . . Lord, teach us how to pray."

Jesus therefore taught them a marvelous prayer —his own prayer, which he instituted just as he instituted the sacraments and the Church. He trained them to say "Father" and bade them pray in his name, in the name of the Son, like sons. That day, he gave us all a filial prayer, wholly intent on the Father and his glory —a prayer that rivets our attention first on the kingdom of God and his holiness, a prayer that leaped up from the heart of the Son and could never again rise straight and true and compelling except from hearts in which he repeats it.

Any authentic prayer is filial; for that reason, it's the work of grace, which makes us sons. It's an act of faith, hope and charity. Going beyond all words and concepts, it's the fruit of inspiration, for we've received "the spirit of sons, and it makes us cry out, 'Abba, Father!' "[1] This is the fundamental disposition in which all prayer must be rooted: our prayer can't be Christian unless we believe in the Father and call out to him as our Father.

[1] Rom. 8, 15.

Blameworthy, then, are all prayers dictated by lack of confidence. When, on the storm-tossed lake, the apostles shouted, "Save us, Lord, we are going down!" Jesus upbraided them: "Why are you so frightened, you men of little faith?"[2] All the same, he calmed the winds and the sea for them. The apostles obtained the miracle they wanted, but they would have seen a far greater one (and, instead, they missed it forever) if they had let him rest and learned thereby that he can save even while sleeping.

To us, also, he often seems asleep, forever testing our faith. And yet God always grants our prayers. He has said so, and Jesus has repeated it time and again. In all sincerity, parents tell a child, "We'd do anything for you, we'd give you anything." But precisely because they love him, they mustn't satisfy his caprices. They want to give him something better than he's asking for. Consequently, they have to wait till he has thought things over and prepared himself to benefit from what he'll receive. They also have to measure out their gift wisely so that it may be a daily bread, a father's bread, and not the supply with which prodigals run away, convinced they can get along by themselves. So, too, God always hears our prayers, but not as or when we like. He wants us to have deep faith.

Advent opens with the richly symbolic story of Zechariah, Saint John the Baptist's father. For years and years, he had been imploring God for a son, but God had refused. At least, that's what Zechariah

---

[2] Mt. 8, 25 and Lk. 8, 24.

thought as the open wound in his heart festered. He kept praying, of course, since he was a religious man, a priest, a high priest; he continued to discharge his duties and carry out his functions, but he had lost confidence in God. Even though his lips still moved in prayer, his soul was numb. When finally an angel appeared and announced, "Your prayer has been heard," Zechariah answered, "Impossible!" But God had, in fact, heard him. From the very beginning of his first prayer, Zechariah had been answered: he'd have a son, and this son would be a living miracle—a prophet, the greatest prophet of the Old Testament, and the precursor of the Messiah. However, since Zechariah hadn't been heard when and as he wanted, he had stopped trusting but somehow kept praying though he had no more faith in prayer. He prayed but refused to believe it did any good.

If I understand Zechariah at all, it's because of one of my former pupils whose father, an unbeliever, was critically ill. One evening when this boy returned to school, he said to me, "Father, this afternoon a priest, an old friend of Dad's, came to see him. They spent a lot of time together and, when the priest came out, he said, 'Peter, you should be happy: your father just went to confession.' " Before I had a chance to comment on his good news, he looked up at me as if tormented by an ever-recurring question and asked, "But, Father, do you think that means Dad is really converted?" Sensing a real difficulty in his tone of voice, I tried to reason with him calmly. His father, I said, was a sincere man and would never have gone to confession if he hadn't believed in it. "Why, no—of course not!" he answered.

"But, you see, I've been praying for this since I was seven, and now I just can't believe it's so." Since his first communion, for eight long years now, he had prayed for his father's conversion and, in the fervor of his young faith, felt sure he'd obtain it. But as the years passed and his father remained unconverted, the boy's faith burned less brightly. He still prayed, but only from habit and from fear lest his incredulity show and harm someone. Actually, he had given up hope and was the last to believe in his father's conversion. Still, God had heard him from the first moment of that first prayer, which was the result only of divine inspiration. But because it hadn't been answered when he wanted or the way he wanted, he had ceased to believe in the power of prayer and hadn't bothered to discover how he had already been heard.

Even Mary and Jesus were heard this way—quite otherwise than they had expected, far beyond what they had asked. Mary wanted to consecrate herself entirely to God. For that, she'd renounce motherhood and, with it, the proud possibility of bearing the Messiah. Instead, God heard her by putting a child in her arms, a child who was God and to whom she'd consecrate herself in a way she had never foreseen. And Jesus? "During his life on earth, he offered up prayer and entreaty, aloud and in silent tears, to the one who had the power to save him out of death, and he submitted so humbly that his prayer was heard. Although he was Son, he learnt to obey through suffering."[3] What he had begged for was deliverance from suffering; what

[3] Heb. 5, 7-8.

he obtained was infinitely better: the strength to obey
and to accept his passion and death.

We think that praying and wresting gifts from
God is a long, painful process; but he finds it far longer
and more painful to get us to accept them. A priest
spends his whole life helping people understand and accept God's way of answering them. We pray and make
offerings, we assume responsibilities and say frightful
things like "May your will be done! May your kingdom
come!" One minute later, we forget all about it—sure
we won't be heard, convinced God is inert, distracted or
indifferent. But he's faithful to his word and does what
we ask. If we offer ourselves, he accepts; if we beg, he
gives; if we knock, he opens the door. God is terrible.
We'd rather he were a good sport, a "regular guy." He
ought to be satisfied with the gesture: after all, we offer
ourselves, and that should be enough. But no, it isn't
enough for God. When we offer ourselves, he accepts
us, plunders us, takes everything—and then some; and
we tremble and weep, as we moan, "Let me have that,
at least." But that, too, he claims and carries off, till
we're left bare as a bone, pure as a choice offering.
Unyieldingly he exacts everything we promise him.

Strange as it may seem, that's how he proves to
be a father in us. If a father is one who calls children
into existence, God is the supreme Father. Have you
ever wondered why it hurts so much to pray? Because
praying is being born to another life, and being born is
painful. What with all the blood rushing into our stif-
fened limbs and the air suddenly inflating our crumpled
lungs, we cry out in protest. But here, it's our heavenly

Father bestowing life on us, and he alone knows what a blessing it is.

When we pray, we start to see things as God does, we enter into his views; but, above all, his life enters into us and carries us along. Then we understand that, since it isn't we who are praying, we should proceed timidly, fitting our inept words to the prayer that rises from him. As we continue, they'll change of themselves and the right ones will haltingly find the corresponding notes in this melody. And sooner or later—by dint of attention, humility and silence—God's muffled prayer within us will ring out on our lips.

Sooner or later, too—after much thinking and believing, not in what we're seeking after, but in the Father we're seeking it from—we'll eventually learn what we ought to pray for. Let's not be so arrogant as to tell him what he should give us. Rather, let's listen as he tells us what we should ask him in the course of a loving conversation where, as men, we propose and he, as God, freely disposes of our heart. We'll have to pay long and close attention; but if we're to let ourselves be convinced, he's the one who must teach us.

Perhaps this is how our prayer will sound for a while: "Father, teach me how to knock. Right now, I'm closed up within myself. I'm on the wrong side of the door and vaguely remember there's another side, but I can't go beyond and I'm not even sure I care to. It's so much easier to stay on this side. . . . Deep down, I want to batter at this door, give it a few good blows, and bruise and gash myself on it so that I can always exhibit—against you—the hate-filled testimony of my futile attempts. But, as for the door itself, I have absolutely no hope it'll ever open, and I really don't want it to. . . .

"Lord, it's difficult learning how to knock properly. Knocking means communicating with someone else, hoping, waiting and answering—all things I don't know how to do. Instead of dwelling morosely on myself, alternately pitying and vexing my ego and worrying for the sake of worrying, I must think of someone else and remember that there actually is someone else —a Being I can speak to, who waits and listens, hoping I'll show some sign of confidence and make some gesture of friendship. . . .

"Lord, I know that, in a sense, the door's already open. When I decide to turn around and raise my hand to it; when (with tears in my eyes and some measure of peace and humility in my heart) I go to knock timidly, holding back somewhat in order to intensify my faith, just grazing the door so that I won't offend the attentive ear that's listening for me and so that my knocking may be truly a sign instead of a clattering of bone on wood—then, I'll find the door open and push it a trifle wider with my finger. Yet I'll keep from opening it too fast, so as to 'prepare myself a bit' to meet you, for you're much more eager to open up than I am to enter. At that moment, I'll realize that I'm not yet ready: I hate the gift I've been soliciting, and I secretly refuse it while reproaching you for not granting it to me. . . .

"Lord, teach me how to knock; make me understand that I have no business telling you how to open up. I'm the one who shuts the door. I barricade myself behind all sorts of doors and drive myself mad there. Show me how to calm down, to stay still for a minute, to breathe deeply, listen, and awake from my nightmares—in your arms. . . .

"Lord, I'm knocking only because you help me to. On second thought, isn't it rather you who knock and I who won't open the door?"

Pray Long, but with Few Words

In Saint Luke's Gospel, Jesus tells a parable "about the need to pray continually and never lose heart."[1] God doesn't like prayers that end. If prayer is his life in us, and if it's the expression of the desires of faith, hope and charity that he unceasingly elicits in our souls, it obviously has to be continual.

But, first, we mustn't think it's an endless declamation. There's no need to "babble as the pagans do, for they think that by using many words they will make themselves heard."[2] Actually, too many words kill prayer. Take, for example, a child who goes and sits quietly in a corner of his parish church. The silence soon fills him with peace, and the all-pervasive presence nourishes and uplifts him. Perfectly content, he remains silent. Then a grown-up enters, spots him and asks, "What are you doing?"
"Nothing."
"Say a Hail Mary, then."
So he recites it and leaves immediately because the words have killed prayer. They kill us, too, whereas realities feed us. So do words if they're real; but, all too often, they're empty and so drained of meaning that we say them without thinking. They weary us without bearing fruit.

Our words hide things instead of revealing them.

[1] Lk. 18, 1.
[2] Mt. 6, 7.

21

Say we come upon a flower, a bird or an insect we've never seen before. We observe it intently and are amazed at what we discover. Then, unfortunately, we remember its name—an old, familiar one. From that moment on, we stop observing the object; because we think we know it, we stop knowing it. The word has screened the reality from view. This happens especially in prayer. Nowhere else do we use words so much and think of them so little. "O my God, I firmly believe . . . With firm confidence I hope . . . I love you above all things . . . I wash my hands in innocence. . . ." Yes, we say all those things, but do we ever stop to ponder what they mean? Péguy didn't dare recite the Our Father, since he understood what he was saying: "Forgive us our trespasses as we forgive those who trespass against us" and "May your kingdom come!" How about us? Do we really long for the coming of God's kingdom? Are we looking forward to the Parousia, the end of the world, when his reign will be universal? Indeed, not: we want a little more time to breathe, to do what we like, even to sin. Or again, when we say "Father," what exactly do we think of? Our earthly fathers? Ourselves and the kind of fathers we'd be? Or our heavenly Father and what he's like if, thoroughly evil though we are, we can still manage to be such good fathers?

To pray, we have to relearn words and come to appreciate their value; we have to pray long, but with few words. That's how Jesus prayed. Though he continued right through the night, all the prayers we have from him are extremely short. He simply repeated them over and over. We, too, must do that: pray for a long time, until the words take on significance and we say them intelligently.

We have to say the Our Father very slowly, repeating each phrase again and again: "Father . . . on earth . . . forgive us. . . ." And sometimes we have to stop saying it, not daring to proceed, because we notice we don't mean it. Then it's a matter of pausing and learning it all over again as we try to sense what we should think and feel in order to say it well. We have to linger over the same idea until we've exhausted its power, until it has ceased to torment and transform us because we've finally become what we're saying. Each new beginning is like the stroke of a scrub plane on the thick plank of our hardness, our distraction, our unbelief. Every thrust slices off a thin shaving. How many will it take for us to break through?

Secondly, prayer doesn't require words at all. In Christianity, God has ceased being a word in order to become a reality, a presence. The Word was made flesh for us so that religion could be, not cerebral, but simple. It would have been much too complicated if we couldn't have known God without syllogizing or believed in him without inventing him first. So, fashioning a religion for the lowly and wanting prayer to be easy and within our reach, he gave us his body to pray. The revelation of God, the manifestation of God, the new and eternal covenant which gives us power over him, consists in this: that with our own eyes we've seen, with our own ears heard, and with our own hands touched the Word, who is life.[3] God has made prayer some-

[3] See 1 Jn. 1, 1.

thing joyful and free by liberating it from words. That's what the Incarnation is about. And it's unceasing; it continues in the sacraments, which are the body, the flesh, the voice and the hands of Jesus perpetuated down to our day so that he may reach out to us and we to him. The Incarnation is God entering into us through all our senses, God taken as food and drink, God invading us by the road that's at once easiest, most direct, most traveled and best fitted to our nature and our capacities. Can prayer be so difficult, then?

Here's what I mean. In his crib, Jesus looked like an ordinary baby—just one more child, with nothing special about him. The whole problem lay in seeing beyond appearances. Mary and Joseph had to look at him, close their eyes and tell themselves who he was, look again a bit closer and with greater faith, shut their eyes again to think of him once more, then open them to see him better. They had to imagine that this was an illusion and that he'd be gone forever when they glanced up, then lift their eyes again and satiate them with wonder and joy. That was prayer. That was all the prayer God required—a look of faith.

The same thing later. On the surface, Jesus seemed just another man, and people elbowed him for thirty years without realizing he wasn't. Then, Saint John the Baptist and a few others, inspired by heaven, started to see him as he truly was, and began to listen and speak to him accordingly. Or consider the woman who had been suffering from a hemorrhage for twelve years. While the crowds merely gawked at him, milling about and even jostling him, she alone understood and thought, "If I can only touch his cloak I shall be well again."[4] She alone touched it with faith; she prayed as she ought and was cured. Yet the poor soul had only one try, one chance. How happy she would have been, how confident, if she'd had Jesus near her for an hour or two or three—or as long as she chose!

But that's our special privilege. We should fairly burst with hope and ardor at the thought of so many Masses where we hear "This is my body" and then see and touch Jesus, so many feasts and prayers, so many confessions and communions in store for us. (Which will be the decisive one? . . .) Think of the countless churches and chapels, too, where we should kiss the floor and reverently touch the altar steps or our own bench; for these things are Jesus, they're his cloak and the floor his feet walk on, they're his body and wounds and voice and presence extended all the way down to us. What happiness to say, "Here he is! I don't have to look any further—my pilgrimage is over at last. Jesus is here for good, and so am I." We needn't worry: he won't leave before we're cured. But how about us? Will we stay that long?

Since God is among us here and now, we should shout for joy inwardly and venture a glance, a word, a kiss; then stop and restrain ourselves, the better to realize who he is and what we're doing; and, after, start over again, prudently and timidly, choked with joy and shame and filled with an overpowering sense of our good fortune.

[4] Mt. 9, 21.

God has given us his body. He has become someone we can touch, someone we can hold on to and huddle up against as we bask secure in his love. Here he is before us, where we can constantly raise our eyes to him and close them again—opening them to see him more clearly, closing them to know him more deeply, reopening them to experience the joyful shock of finding he's still here, and closing them once more to remind ourselves of who he is and why we should be so happy.

That's exactly what the old peasant used to do as he sat alone in an empty church hour after hour. When the Curé d'Ars asked him, "What can you possibly be telling God all this time?" he answered, "Nothing. I just look at him, and he looks at me."

There are days when we can't do a thing. At such times, our only course is to remember that the Holy Spirit himself "expresses our plea in a way that could never be put into words, and God who knows everything in our hearts knows perfectly well what he means."[5] We merely have to associate ourselves with him, consent, answer "Amen" to this Mass which is too complicated for us, and rely on him for everything we ourselves can't do.

As for distractions, we must pull ourselves together and begin afresh every time we notice them. We're not expected to go on unflaggingly, but only to start over humbly. As a Hindu sage once said, "We

[5] Rom. 8, 26-27.

can't stop birds from flying around our head, but we can prevent them from building their nests in our hair."

Since God is the only important being in the universe, since he's our wellspring and the very air we breathe, and since he's ultimately going to be the object of our eternal activity, then we can have no other purpose in this life but to learn how to live and breathe in him. God isn't a last resort in case of accident. Too many Christians look on him as pilots do on their parachute: good if needed, but better if they can get along without. "Yet in fact . . . it is in him that we live, and move, and exist."[6]

If Jesus felt the need of praying—often, right through the night—in order to glorify the Father and renew and strengthen himself, how could we ever survive without prayer?

We must learn to endure hours of tedium in God's presence. All we can do on those days is gently complain to him about ourselves, affectionately bemoaning our boredom, our unfaithfulness and our miserable character. We should humbly admit that we'd rather be elsewhere and that, if it were up to us, we wouldn't have come in the first place or would already have left.

It was a weary prayer that saved the world. One whole night through, Jesus prayed a prayer of desolation. He would have preferred being elsewhere, too, far

[6] Acts 17, 27-28.

from the bitter cup he had to drink. He suffered from weariness enough to die, more than we'll ever suffer from it or from the desire to escape and do our own will.

Our wearied prayer will save the world and us. After these long periods of boredom, we'll notice that our soul has come to life, disciplined itself and grown strong in the struggle. Immense areas of our being now lying fallow, savannas and steppes so far uncharted, have suddenly appeared in a burst of sunlight; our interior dimensions have broadened prodigiously, and we're astounded at everything that has begun to people us.

Because we've been interminably bored in God's presence, we've learned to know and love him. For that's what love is: making a choice and adhering to it, not yielding to the intermittences of the heart but remaining steadfast despite boredom. We never love more or come closer to God than after endless hours of tedium spent with him. We're like a child who thinks he's bored as he plays by his mother's side but who, when she's called away, realizes nothing was dearer to him than that long weariness. Newman says that the religious services that sickness, care and turmoil keep us from relishing; those that weary our fickle heart though we acknowledge their sacredness; those that we find too long, dread before they begin and wish we could end as they drag on—those very services, we understand later, are filled with God's presence. How can we be so blind to our best interests? We rush out, inhale the first breath of fresh air with avidity and relief; and then, in a flash, we sense what we're missing, what we've turned our back on, and we know we were never happier than the whole time we felt so bored. Or we doze off like the exiled Jacob, who slept on a stone and, on awakening, remembered he had seen angels and the Lord, who manifested himself through them.

To pray is to die and be born again: to die in a whole sphere of ourselves where we're altogether too alive, but dry, agitated and sterile; and to be born at a dizzying depth where our blind soul begins to stir, blood starts circulating through our numbed being once more, and movement returns to our paralyzed limbs. That hurts, and the pain persists; but it's the pain we feel on being born or on coming back to life.

Meeting Christ in Prayer

Often, our life is only the fulfillment of some forgotten prayer. What we're suffering and rebelling against now, we asked for and offered up in the past. We've merely forgotten about it, concluding that our prayers went unheard once again because they weren't answered on the spot. Yet God exacts from us everything we've promised him; he believes we're sincere, and he accomplishes what we've earnestly desired. We've sometimes said with all our heart, "May your will be done; may your kingdom come"; and now that we're receiving our reply, we don't recognize it. I've often seen people so distressed that they could neither understand nor accept their situation. But when I asked them, "Are you sure you never prayed for this, never offered it up?" they suddenly remembered an act of oblation made long before, an old prayer which they didn't realize they had meant so completely but which the Lord had accepted and just recently answered.

The place for these deepmost meetings with the Lord is prayer. That's where, in the days of his earthly life, the Son used to find his Father. That's where we find him whenever we've lost him, whenever we're about to lose him; that's where we become his sons again, as Jesus did ever more fully.

People recognized Jesus better when he prayed than when he worked wonders. Miracles often left the spectators sunk in their material interests ("You

31

are . . . looking for me . . . because you had all the
bread you wanted to eat"[1]) rather than transported into
the world of God. But when he returned from prayer,
some began to surmise who he might be. "I do nothing
of myself: what the Father has taught me is what I
preach; he who sent me is with me, and has not left me
to myself, for I always do what pleases him." It was
during prayer that the Father taught him; during prayer
that Jesus rediscovered with certainty that he was never
alone, that the Father was near him and was pleased
with him. "As he was saying this," Saint John adds,
"many came to believe in him."[2] Jesus spoke these filial
words with such warmth and joy and peace that his listeners began to feel like orphans hearing the echo of a
loving and intimate dialogue. They saw that something
essential was lacking: meant to be sons, they had lived
without the Father.

While Jesus spoke, "as he was saying this," sonship appeared to them as the only possible, the only
real human condition. They couldn't go on living without something so vital, and they couldn't help believing
in someone who offered to introduce them to it. "How
beautiful it would be if there were a God for me to love
and obey!" sighed Coventry Patmore before his conversion. But his mere openness to the idea of a God to
whom he could be a son filled Patmore with such
gladness that he believed. There had to be a God since
he now knew that, for him, there was no other reality
but sonship.

[1] Jn. 6, 26.
[2] Jn. 8, 28-30

The most wretched orphan is the one who imagines he has everything he needs. Let him once see a real family, and he immediately plumbs the depths of his poverty and misfortune. At first, it pains him; but if he learns that he's been introduced to this happy life, to this atmosphere of mutualness and spontaneity so that he may enter into it forever, and that being adopted depends entirely on him—then his sorrow changes into wonder. The revelation was an invitation.

That's the experience shared by those who saw Jesus pray. Nothing could have been more impressive than that retransfiguration, that return to the wellspring from which he emerged remade, renewed and restored both to himself and to his filial condition.

It'd be a serious mistake to think Jesus was always the same: always calm and impassible, always in command of self and others, always capable of transmitting a steady divine charge beneath his indefatigable human exterior. The logical conclusion would be that if he prayed, he did it only to give us good example. But Jesus never put on a show.

The Incarnation isn't a pious make-believe meant to comfort us. Jesus is a real man—"true God and true man." During his mortal life, he was as sensitive to the people and things around him as any other human; he had the nerves of a human, the temperament of a human and the patience of a human (that is, limited patience). On certain occasions, he was overwhelmed by anxiety: "Now my soul is troubled. What shall I say: Father, save me from this hour? But it was for this

very reason that I have come to this hour. Father, glorify your name!"[3] Only after praying was he able to
pull himself together and face "this hour" of anguish,
loathing and darkness: "My Father, if it is possible, let
this cup pass me by. Nevertheless, let it be as you, not
I, would have it."[4] At times, he was annoyed: "Men of
little faith . . . do you not yet understand? . . . How
could you fail to understand that I was talking about
bread?"[5] Irritated: "Faithless and perverse generation!
How much longer must I be among you and put up
with you?"[6] Impatient: "Are your minds closed? Have
you eyes that do not see, ears that do not
hear? . . . Are you still without perception?"[7] And
discouraged: "My soul is sorrowful to the point of
death."[8] Some days, he was at the end of his rope,
exhausted by the sniping and badgering of all those
mediocre, covetous men who hedged him about with
their petty preoccupations.

When he felt submerged, blocked and cut off
from his own world like this, "he would always go off
to some place where he could be alone and pray."[9]
He'd climb some hilltop or withdraw to a sequestered
spot (a "desert") in order to breathe deeply and purify
the atmosphere, to steep himself anew in the thought of
his Father, to contact the presence too much noise and
bustling had drowned out, to let himself be filled and

[3] Jn. 12, 27-28.
[4] Mt. 26, 39.
[5] Mt. 16, 8-9. 11.
[6] Lk. 9, 41.
[7] Mk. 9, 17-18. 21.
[8] Mk. 14, 34.
[9] Lk. 5, 16.

nourished by the Father and so become his Son again, singlehearted, composed and loving. Gradually, his true likeness returned and shone through his features; from the depths of him, the fountainhead sprang up once more; the Spirit reinvaded his whole weary human body and integrated his entire being.

When Jesus came back, no one could explain why he was so beautiful, so impressive, so luminous; no one could describe the peace that stole over them all. But the apostles said to one another, "He's been praying. If only we could, too! . . . Lord, teach us how to pray."[10]

By praying as he did, we'll find him again and, together with him, the Father—provided we, too, are seeking Another, and not ourselves. For prayer isn't a matter of "finding ourselves" and reinvigorating our loud, selfish, detestable ego; or nursing the wounds inflicted on our self-sufficiency in recent clashes; or even reminding a forgetful God of what our "special" personality needs in order to blossom.

On the contrary, it's simply a matter of dying and being born. The whole of Christianity is a participation in the death and resurrection of Christ, but prayer associates us with both most intimately. Just as there's a kind of devil that only prayer can rout, so there's a kind of death that only prayer can effect. To pray is to die to our ideas, our misgivings, our sloth, our selfish desires; and be born to God's ideas, to his

[10] See Lk. 11, 1.

will, to a love and faith that can spring from his heart
alone.

But we always try to leave well before that happens. If we stayed for any length of time—good heavens, we'd start viewing things the way God does. "I can
only judge as I hear,"[11] said Jesus; and if we prayed for
a while, we'd begin to hear the Father like him. We'd
see that nasty blow, that unbearable privation, that
"calamity" for the graces and blessings they really are,
and eventually come to rejoice in them. Then we'd have
nothing left of our town—not even an opinion, not even
the right to complain. As things stand now, it's no fun
but at least we have something: *our* sacrifice, *our* merits
and *our* determination to hold fast.

The will is like the beam of a balance. When the
scalepans are uneven, we can equalize them in two
ways: either grab the beam (and destroy everything) or
redistribute the weights in the pans. When we come to
prayer, our scalepan is extremely heavy and God's is so
light that it's lost in the clouds high above us. We're
crushed, obsessed by mountains of anger, disgust, mediocrity, pessimism and impurity—mountains we absolutely can't budge. It's enough if we stay there and pray
awhile. We start by grumbling, and that's good—certainly better than putting on an act. We'd be lying if we
parroted sublime sentiments like "I want whatever you
want. . . ." They're simply not true. Better to say,
"Lord, leave me alone and don't talk to me about your
will. I don't want any part of it. For one thing, I'm not

[11] See Jn. 5, 30.

up to it; it's too hard for me. I'd break down right away, as I've already done so often. Let's talk about something else." But how can we talk about anything else very long? And how can we continue to talk all alone? God replies. While we're speaking, he works in us; he raises our mediocrity, charms our disgust, and extinguishes our anger. If we stay long enough, we're suddenly astonished to find ourselves at peace. Everything has changed, the mountain has disappeared, our problems have faded away. All is simple now, and we're content. "Lord, it's good to be here. Your will is sweet, and so's the life you've prepared for me. How could I be so afraid of it a while ago, how could I think it so bitter? Lord, I'm glad your will is going to be done!"

Imagine that: the pulverizing burden, the insurmountable obstacle, was nothing at all. We were just looking at it from the wrong angle, tackling it the wrong way; it plagued us because we refused to face it. Like Tobias, who had to take the monstrous fish by the gills, we had only to seize our problem with both hands and dare look at it closer with God, for everything to go well. From the outside, it seemed horrible. But, without our knowing quite how, he called us, pushed and guided us; we let him do as he pleased, soon found ourselves on the inside—"where [we] would rather not go"[12]—and were at peace. "Shoulder my yoke and learn from me. . . . Yes, my yoke is easy and my burden light."[13]

[12] See Jn. 21, 18.
[13] Mt. 11, 29-30

God consistently cheats us of our dreams in order to teach us hope. There's a world of difference between disappointment and refusal. He makes us renounce something only to meet Someone. Unwilling to give us less than himself, he discourages us from begging his gifts so that we'll seek the Giver.

It's not surprising that his extraordinary generosity baffles those who approach him. Since they come with timid, trivial requests, they're almost always put off at first. In reading the Gospels, have you ever noticed that the Lord invariably starts by vetoing the miracles asked of him? This confirms the impression we have that our own prayers often remain fruitless. But have you also noticed that, in the end, he always rewards those who persevere unshaken?

Even the Blessed Virgin, at the wedding feast in Cana, wasn't heard immediately.[14] Though, in her compassion, she whispered, "They have no wine," Jesus seemingly rejected her mediation. "Woman," he said, "why turn on me? My hour has not come yet." Fortunately, she didn't become discouraged, like us, but waited, both acquiescent and trustful. "Do whatever he tells you," she bade the servants, because she knew right well he'd say something further.

Lazarus' sisters, Martha and Mary, sent Jesus this message: "Lord, the man you love is ill."[15] (What a perfect prayer for us to say in periods of suffering and

14 See Jn. 2, 1-10.
15 See Jn. 11, 1-44.

aridity!) Now, as Saint John stresses, "Jesus loved Martha and her sister and Lazarus, yet when he learned that Lazarus was ill he stayed where he was for two more days." Two days—enough time for a long prayer, enough time to die, enough time to let Lazarus die. For the sisters had requested a mere cure, but Jesus knows that we need nothing short of resurrection.

The Canaanite woman serves as another example. Imploring her daughter's cure, she kept shouting, "Sir, Son of David, take pity on me!"[16] At first, Jesus didn't answer a word. Still, she wouldn't let his harshness disconcert her. (And neither should we; for, though it may offend us, it also reveals a deeper plan.) He felt a sort of nostalgia for pagans; he loved their freshness, their spontaneity and their sensitivity to God; and he contrasted them favorably with his own people.[17] If he seemed to brush this pagan aside, then, he wanted only to elicit from her a mightier faith than it takes to request miracles.

"Give her what she wants," his disciples urged, "because she is shouting after us." Even if they were interceding in her behalf, as some exegetes maintain, the motive was very selfish. Let's face it: half the time, it's our vices that furnish the driving power behind our so-called virtues.

Jesus replied, "I was sent only to the lost sheep of the House of Israel." How cold that must have

16 See Mt. 15, 21-18.
17 See Lk. 10, 13-15.

sounded to the Canaanite. Jesus didn't even acknowledge her cry but answered only indirectly through this
remark addressed to his followers, who hadn't exactly
made the privileged House of Israel sympathetic. The
normal reaction would have been, "Oh, they're all the
same! Everything for themselves. As if we weren't just
as good. . . ." But she thought no such thing. Instead,
the Gospel goes on, "the woman had come up and was
kneeling at his feet. 'Lord,' she said, 'help me.' "

Even then Jesus didn't grant her prayer, for she
hadn't yet climbed as high as he wanted. Knowing her
more fully than she herself or anyone else did, he
planned a far closer communion between her and himself, and saw what heights of faith, humility and trust
she could scale if he helped her. There was danger, of
course, since we often turn away resentful when, with
the same loving audacity, he offers us the same exigent
closeness; but there's worse danger in hearing our
requests too soon.

Like us when we first start praying, she came to
ask Jesus for a favor to take back home with her, a
miracle with which to run far away from him. Jesus, on
the contrary, hoped she wouldn't want to return home,
but detach herself from what she was asking and cling
to him to whom she was praying, and agree not to go
back to her own people but become one of his forever.
For this, he needed a little time, a little patience. So he
made another statement, even more caustic, more bru-
tal than the first: "It is not fair to take the children's
food and throw it to the house-dogs."

Because she was undoubtedly free of pride and skepticism, she went beyond the surface of Jesus' words and perceived in them his immense expectancy. She knew they weren't an answer, but a question; not a refusal, but an invitation. When a professor poses a difficult question, the poorer students immediately conclude he wants to flunk them, and they hate him for it. But there are always a few whose faces light up with gratitude and joy; for they realize that if they find the answer, he'll be even prouder and happier than they, and the relationship between them will become even closer. In the same spirit, the Canaanite retorted, "Ah yes, sir; but even house-dogs can eat the scraps that fall from their master's table." With affectionate malice, she used Christ's own argument to get the better of him.

Quick-witted and respectful, humble and confident, she was completely open to God. They smiled at one another: they had enjoyed a good joke together and would be friends forever after. Without jeopardizing her now, he could grant what she wanted. Gifts do no harm between friends, but between strangers they obligate people instead of liberating them and expressing affection. There was no more danger of losing her, of having her run off with her treasure. For her treasure, from that day on, was the memory of that instant when he had reached out to her and called and waited till, from deep within, she produced this being whom she herself didn't know and by whom both were equally dazzled: "Woman, you have great faith."

One last example.[18]   The court official whose son lay dying in Capernaum was called to the same self-transcendence.

"Hearing that Jesus had arrived in Galilee from Judea, he went and asked him to come and cure his son, as he was at the point of death." It's easy to imagine how fast and anxiously he traveled. His family expected the worst and had lost all hope when, suddenly, rumor spread that Jesus, the man from whom miracles flowed like water from a spring, had just reached Cana. Everyone around the official had encouraged him to go, and now his wife was waiting back home, listening for every footstep along the road. He had promised her he'd bring Jesus back, no matter what.

At first glance, the Lord's answer to this desperate father seems cold and disdainful: "So you will not believe unless you see signs and portents!" We get the idea that Jesus was continuing a polemic begun with others—the hardened Pharisees—without bothering to notice what was new and simple about this stranger's approach. But the man didn't enter into a discussion, since he hadn't come to convince Jesus but to stir the goodness in which he placed all his confidence. He merely repeated his touching plea, "Sir, come down before my child dies." Far from yielding, however, Jesus imposed an agonizing trial on him. "Go home," he said, "your son will live."

To us, those words sound like a promise, be-

[18] See Jn. 4, 46-54.

cause we know the story; but to the official, they rang like a death sentence. Only one thing on earth mattered at that moment: to bring Jesus back with him and have him loose the prodigious power that healed anyone who touched the hem of his cloak. Yet Jesus refused to go and signified that the father would be heard, not in the way he had expected, but in a way that required infinitely deeper faith. Significantly, Saint John's narrative doesn't contain a solitary word of reply—just the command "Go home, your son will live." As if knocked senseless, the nobleman reeled under the blow and said nothing. "Go home. . . ." He couldn't insist and yet was afraid to leave: to insist would be to lack faith, but to leave would be to throw away his last chance. For a long time, he stood there hesitating.

Nothing, he thought, could have been harder than going back alone, with a promise that was more like an order. He'd have to walk for hours, all night, holding fast to this word in which he dared neither believe nor disbelieve. He pictured himself coming home, and his disappointed wife asking, "Didn't you meet the prophet?"

"Yes, I saw him."

"And you didn't bring him back?"

"No, I'm alone."

"Well, then, you may as well know the truth: our boy is dead."

"It's my fault. I held salvation in my hands and I let it go."

Finally, the Lord overcame his resistance, and he left without saying a word. What was demanded of him lay so near the extreme limit of his strength that he couldn't do any more than obey. Silently, he set out, living only on "what Jesus had said." He had come, like each of us, full of confidence in what he was asking; and he went away, as we should, full of confidence in the God to whom he had spoken.

The poor man went his way alone, not knowing whether this was the stupidest or the sublimest moment in his life and not allowing himself to judge. Thus, when his servants met him with the news that his boy was alive, he immediately asked when the child had begun to recover. From this we see what interested him above all, what was most important to him now: no longer what he had obtained, but how he had obtained it and from whom. His question concerned, not his son, but Jesus—Jesus, who had required such faith of him and brought forth such confidence. Only God could have transformed him so. "And he and all his household believed."

Our best prayers, those where we meet the Lord, are the ones which pain us most at the start. "Man cannot see [God] and live."[19] Authentic prayer tears us away from ourselves and pushes us into the opposing camp, but we so cleave to every last vestige of self that we must perpetually beg, "Remake me, O God, and force me to cooperate with you."

To pray is to expose ourselves to God as we do to heat or sunlight. In seeking out Jesus, the royal of-

---

[19] Exod. 33, 20.

ficial exposed himself to him and was profoundly changed. From then on, there was room in his heart for the metamorphosing revelation of the true God, not the healer whose services he had come to requisition. If we really want God to hit on target, we should start our prayer life by imitating the soldier who pokes his head out of the foxhole, under a hail of bullets, to see whether it's time to be killed. For praying means running the risk, or taking the chance, of being done to death. "Lord, when will you ever destroy that dull, irksome, shortsighted being whose ideas estrange me from yours, whose desires run counter to yours, whose activity impedes yours? I'd so want to concur in your plans for me; but, to do that, you know I've got to be emptied of self first. When will you rid me of myself for good? See, I'm raising my head and looking at you, I'm invoking you, I'm provoking you. Isn't this the day for me to die?"

Time passes, slowly and peacefully, forever renewing both occasion and purpose; and eventually, thanks to this erosive pressure and all this beneficial suffering, a strange vivification occurs. We thought we were dying, and we start to live. God gives us life while putting us to death: incomprehensibly, we begin to love and give thanks in the very part of ourselves that we judged fit only to die; our marrowless bones spring back to life; and grace flows unobstructed through our mortified flesh. We'll never finish, never have enough of being slain like this.

Prayer and the Laity

For half a century now, the popes have been striving to create, to re-create, a laity. Since the advent of Protestantism, there had been so much insistence on the rights, powers and importance of the hierarchy that *Church* and *hierarchy* became synonymous. The twentieth century is rediscovering that the clergy exists to serve the laity and that without the laity there's no Church.

But some habits die hard, and declericalized priests often run into laymen who are more Catholic than the pope and more clerical than their pastors. When one speaks to most laymen about their "vocation,"[1] they promptly suspect he wants to steer them toward the cloister. They're unaware of their Christian vocation, though it's so much more essential than a religious vocation. When one asks about their spiritual life, they answer, "I pray every night and receive every Sunday"—which is like inquiring about their work and being told, "I eat three square meals a day." After all, a layman's spiritual life is his professional life, his civic and family life. All he does in church is nourish his faith and charity so as to live them on the job, at home and in the community.

Let's not deceive ourselves: we don't love God more than we love our state in life; we don't respect

[1] See Eph. 1, 3-6.

God more than we respect our occupation; we're no closer to God than we are to our family, our neighbors, our fellow workmen. In other words, we don't love God more than we love his will in our regard, the mission he sends us on, or the persons he has entrusted to us. Every morning at Mass, we solemnly declare, "It is truly right and just, proper and helpful toward salvation, that we *always and everywhere* give thanks to you, O Lord, holy Father, almighty and eternal God." Then we return to what we call our "stupid" job, our "stupid" kitchen, our "stupid" family and neighborhood. Yet that's where God expects us to celebrate *our* Mass; that's where and when we're supposed to give thanks.

Too many husbands and wives excuse their meager spiritual life by saying, "I'm trapped in material things up to my neck." But what are these "material things" if not people to cherish and look after, or chores to be done so we can serve others and prove our love? When a mother asks herself, "What'll I give them for supper today?" she's really asking, "How can I show them once again that I dearly love them?" Now, the spiritual life is just such a life of love, and the only materialism in these duties is our lack of faith and love as we accomplish them.

One of the chief reasons why the laity feels discouraged and demoralized is that, until modern times, the ideal of holiness was entirely preempted by religious. Laymen resigned themselves to a kind of watered-down monasticism because they didn't recognize the sanctifying values proper to their own life in the world. All too often, religious actively fostered this attitude. For example, when a lawyer asked Saint Catherine of Siena to be his spiritual director, she stipulated that he must first leave his wife and abandon his profession.

There's a grain of truth in the quip that, at the Reformation, the Protestants took off with the Holy Spirit and we Catholics stayed behind with the hierarchy. The specificity of ecclesiastical functions, along with the importance of the functionaries, has been so exaggerated that the clergy has stripped laymen of both their priesthood and their responsibility in the Church while monks have monopolized prayer and sometimes holiness itself. The religious life is loudly hailed as a "state of perfection"—which presumably leaves the laity in the state of imperfection, as if one couldn't be a thorough Christian and a thorough layman at the same time, and as if Christ hadn't commanded all of us to be perfect like the Father.

Listen to Jacques Maritain describe this mentality:

> [Laymen's] business is from their material resources to make prosperous, by means of pious foundations, the religious who in exchange win them a way into heaven, whereby all the claims of order will be satisfied.

This way of conceiving a lay humility seems to have been widely enough extended in the sixteenth and seventeenth centuries. It was for this reason that the explanatory catechism of the Dominican Carranza, who

was, moreover, Archbishop of Toledo, was condemned
by the Spanish Inquisition at the direction of the cele-
brated theologian, Melchior Cano. This latter declared
that "it is entirely wrong to claim to give the faithful a
form of religious instruction which is only suitable to
priests. . . . He was equally in arms against the reading of the Gospel in the common tongue . . . and the
saying is attributed to him in a sermon that in his eyes
one of the signs of the approach of Anti-Christ was this
general frequentation of the sacraments."[2]

In our own time, some reputable authors who
want to sound up-to-date still write, "Laymen, also, are
part of the Church," a platitude as laughable as "The
soldiers, also, are part of the army." Without soldiers,
there'd simply be no army; and the bemedaled generals,
all by themselves, would be good only for operettas and
Latin American revolutions. Basically, the structures in
our Church are so ponderous that they dispense or prevent the community from living. Most Catholics have a
proletarian spirit: they subsist off an enterprise that
operates without them.

Even today, what most lay persons lack is pride
and joy: the thrilling awareness that they have a mission and are serving God in their conjugal and professional life. They work courageously and, in general, ex-
cessively—but without gladness. Swamped by some
occupation they deem purely secular, they try to com-
pensate the shameful paganism of it with toilsome and

---

[2] Jacques Maritain, *True Humanism*, translated by Margot
Adamson (New York: Charles Scribner's Sons, 1938), pp.
116-117.

sporadic attempts at prayer. By and large, they underestimate their vocation. They don't understand that God needs them right where they are to carry on his work among men; they don't realize that he has purposely committed this task, this woman or these children to them, and that they're all like the wise and faithful servant who has been appointed to provide for every member of his master's household.[3] God needed someone to make this man or woman happy, to raise these children, to do that particular job; he needed someone to manifest his tenderness and power, his fidelity and joy. And he has chosen them to do it. If only they could see that and take more pride in it! If only they could feel that they're God's "lieutenants"—those who take his place—in their family and especially in their work! There's no calling so lowly but it can and must glorify God and bear witness to him. If the Son spent thirty years sawing and planing in a village workshop; if Mary spent the same thirty years (and how many more after?) cooking, washing and spinning in a hovel; if God needed that cult, that devotion, that liturgy, we shouldn't look for a way out but, rather, be only too glad and proud that we've been chosen to continue offering it to him. If the Son was sent into the world, we should all be overjoyed at being sent there, each morning, to save it like him.[4]

Yet so many laymen feel divided, pulled in two directions and materialized by their work. I know scores of good Christians who've been trying unsuccess-

[3] See Mt. 24, 45.
[4] See Jn. 17, 18.

fully for years to pray ten minutes a day. For them, the only reality is their life as workers—which is exactly like that of any contemporary who doesn't have the faith. Yearning for something like a Truce of God or released time, they try regularly to cut corners here and there so as to have a few minutes for religious exercises, but it doesn't take and they have to keep starting over. The crowd is insensitive and ill-attuned to prayer, and, secretly, they feel rather on the side of the crowd.

The trouble is, they haven't been clearly shown the religious value of their work. Whenever one mentions the spiritual life, they eye the cloister with envy instead of looking squarely at their own existence as the place where they're called to sanctify and offer themselves to God. They don't realize what Master they're serving; like soldiers without a flag, they don't know what cause they're defending. Though dispirited and mechanical now, they're courageous and would soon become the best soldiers on earth if they could experience joy in serving their Master. "Come and join in your master's happiness."[5]

Actually, when they think of God, these good people feel like culprits or outcasts. They reproach themselves for dreading recollection, for not praying enough and not attending weekday Mass—all of which is perfectly natural, since they imagine that God disapproves of them, that he's alien to their concerns, and that they'd have to escape from their mode of life (a thing which is obviously impossible) in order to reach

[5] Mt. 25, 21.

him. How could they enjoy meditating on their failures, their remorse, their faults? What satisfaction could they find in thinking of God?

To tell the truth, perhaps there's just one thing missing for them to become perfect Christians: a tiny bit of pride in themselves, the conviction that God is pleased with everything they do for him—even when they're not fully aware of it, a little joy at the thought that he didn't wait but commandeered them before they could dedicate themselves explicitly to his objectives. As I see it, the exact dose of prayer lacking in their life is precisely this uplift of joy, this pride in responsibility, this ever-renewed acceptance, this eucharist of a soul which can say to its Master, "All I have is yours and all you have is mine."[6] Isn't this continual elevation, this burst of gratitude, this thanksgiving for all we've received and, at the same time, this perpetual aspiration to become worthier of it—isn't this the truest prayer? Contemplatives, mystics and religious are the expression of our praise, which overflows to the point of never ending. We therefore recognize ourselves in them: they're the pure image of what we want to become: they're heaven made visible.

I firmly believe that our gear wheels squeak because they need the oil of prayer; and that, once this source has gushed forth, it'll grow more and more powerful. Laymen won't pray till they enjoy praying, till they pray from sheer pleasure now and then. That cry of contentment is what will introduce them to genuine

[6] Jn. 17, 10.

prayer, to prolonged, silent prayer. And when exhaustion, trouble or callosity robs them of the joy that once made their job so dear to them, they'll automatically do like Jesus, who endured our overwork (he didn't even have time to eat), our temptations to impatience, and our disappointments. Like him, they'll go pray.

Jesus, too, experienced those moments when our activity rushes headlong, out of control, and threatens to run away with us. At such times, he'd take his apostles and "[go] off in a boat to a lonely place where they could be by themselves."[7] And there he'd pray. Once peace and love had returned to his heart and he had let the Father inspire him till his face became luminous and gentle again, he'd come back ready for any task and open to all the suffering on earth. To modern laymen also prayer will restore what work has snatched away, but it's the work received from God that will first have taught them prayer. Working is *not* praying, unless our work has become a mission that God entrusts to us and that we accomplish in a spirit of fidelity. Perhaps we have to renounce everything and then accept it all back from God's hands again if we're to fulfill Saint Paul's mandate: "Those who have wives should live as though they had none, and those who mourn should live as though they had nothing to mourn for; those who are enjoying life should live as though there were nothing to laugh about; those whose life is buying things should live as though they had nothing of their own; and those who have to deal with the world should not become engrossed in it."[8] For if we hold

[7] Mk. 6, 32.
[8] 1 Cor. 7, 29-31.

everything from the Lord's hands, then we'll hold to the Lord himself even more than to what he gives us.

There are two vocations: that of the rich young aristocrat ("Sell all that you own . . . then come, follow me"[9]), but also that of the possessed man who, after his cure, begged to be allowed to stay with Jesus but was told, "Go home to your people and tell them all that the Lord in his mercy has done for you."[10] Though the second vocation is more frequent, it, also, is a mission from the Lord. If you don't accept it but always hanker for the first, you leave empty the place Christ has confided to you; and empty it'll stay throughout eternity, since no one can substitute for you. To become a saint, you needn't wait for another calling, a different occupation or even widowhood. You must be religious now—or never. You must get up immediately, go remarry your wife or husband, rebeget your children and resume your lifework, continually reembracing whatever the Lord has willed for you. You have to leave off praying, and go out to all those whom the Lord has committed to you and for whose well-being he has chosen to need you. Lastly, you should make your life an uninterrupted hymn of gratitude that expresses your amazement at the confidence he has placed in you. And whenever this hymn no longer rises from you, whenever you feel dejected and crushed, you must return to him and lay down your burden so that he may give it back to you again, for he shoulders yours and you can't really shoulder any but his.

[9] Lk. 18, 22.
[10] Mk. 5. 19.

Modern Prayer

For most of us, prayer is incredibly difficult, and we have the hardest time being faithful to it. We can't stay quiet in God's presence; we can't stand the silence and the immobility which, alone, would carry us into him.

When it comes to prayer, we're like those young people of today who need a radio to study for exams. Many modern children are so volatile and fidgety that the drone of background music, instead of distracting them, somehow helps them to concentrate. Without this continual flow of sound and the stabilizing, pacifying presence it affords them, they'd suffer so acutely from their affective and spiritual void that they'd dart to the window or run downstairs and find someone to talk to. But once they're snugly wrapped in a comforting blanket of noise, they can manage to sit still.

That's how it is with prayer for most people nowadays. We can't pray five minutes, not because we don't want to (on the contrary, we'd like to pray well), but because we can't concentrate, we can't endure silence or stay put, we can't wait and listen. An uncontrollable nervous impulsion drives us on, involving us in some urgent project, some errand, some function or other—anything as long as we're on the go, as long as we can chatter and get out of praying. Otherwise, we'd have to talk to God; we'd have to stop fibbing and flitting and fretting; we'd have to let him relieve us of this burden we gripe about constantly but hold to more dearly than life.

Well, then, since we're so disinclined to prayer and must be radically reeducated in it, why not begin humbly by drawing near to God, without trying to speak or hear him at first? Why not simply come into his presence; and, because the stillness frightens us, start by living close to him, quite naturally, for long stretches of time? We can arm ourselves with a mental equivalent of radio or of the rosary—a novel, for instance, or some little handiwork. What's so disrespectful about reading a book in church? Suppose our mother is sitting alone in the living room and we come downstairs and read near her—doesn't that please rather than offend her? Besides, the quality of an occupation changes totally according to where we are and the people we're with. I'm afraid some moderns will never learn to converse with God unless they can share at least one of their normal activities with him. Little by little, they'll acquire a taste for his presence and eventually prefer him to any book. The child I mentioned earlier plays close to his mother, intently, without pausing to look at her or speak to her. But let her leave the room for a while, and he soon realizes that his whole joy in playing came from her presence and that they were communing deeply in peaceful and fervent silence, without words or conscious effort. Which is what we ought to do when we pray.

The Rosary

Those who don't recite the rosary allege excellent reasons not to. It's a silly prayer, they maintain: nothing but mechanical repetition, senile mumbling. On the other hand, those who do recite it assure us that it's the most agreeable and encouraging form of prayer, the only fairly prolonged one and, for all of us, the only practical way to pray for any length of time.

I wonder how many of the inspired intelligentsia who scorn the rosary ever keep at their "personal prayer" for fifteen minutes. Yet that's the first requisite for prayer—to stay with it a long time. Only after a while can real prayer well up within us. Generally, we march into church, notify God of what we want, and leave without bothering to listen to him, without consulting him or taking him into account, without giving him time to act, to answer, to change us, or tell us how he sees things and how he intends to grant our request. But the fact is that God has his own ideas and doesn't always share our views. He knows what's good for us much better than we do.

In the Gospels, as we noted earlier, our Lord usually starts by refusing what he's asked for. Strange how he always seems to need time and never says yes right away. He delays, questions and tests; he transforms or reveals the petitioner's inmost heart. His entire strategy is to make us renounce our petty hopes and convert us to the virtue of hope.

What would have happened at Cana if the Blessed Virgin had reacted like us and grumbled, "I knew he wouldn't listen to me. He never does. What's the use of praying anyhow?" On the contrary, with unshaken trust, she persevered in expectancy—a profoundly peaceful expectancy, like the recitation of a rosary—and waited for Jesus to show her how he had already answered. And he did answer, as he always does, far beyond her dreams. She hadn't demanded a miracle but had simply brought a situation to his notice. Maybe she was only suggesting that his apostles be told to decline the next drink. At any rate, she didn't impose her views on God or tell him what to do. She just waited calmly, reciting a sort of rosary.

The same with the Canaanite woman and the royal official we've already discussed. Fortunately, they also held their ground, praying long and insistently; and they remained loyal and open, letting their faith grow till it finally became what God wanted it to be. From the crucible of prayer, each of them emerged a new person. Like them, we must let prayer burn away the slag of self and self's ideas, so as to disengage the purer metal in us. In a word, prayer should make us die to our own life and live God's life.

Now, if all this is true, let's humbly admit that we, too, find prayer difficult and need whatever help we can get. For that reason, let's make the beads slip slowly through our fingers as we murmur the old familiar words. They may seem too old and familiar, but they're inspired words, and it's up to us to recapture their original breath of freshness once again. Let's occupy our mind with this monotonous meditation so that God may gradually reach through to us, accustom us to his ways, win us over to himself and pattern our will on his. Let's say our rosary.

Fact and Fiction
about Prayer and Activity

As soon as we adopt the spirituality of Charles de Foucauld and his Little Brothers, we feel their excruciating paradox: becoming contemplatives out in the world; being permanently delegated to pray in the name of all men and share their living conditions; remaining passionately faithful both to God and to the world; striving to put more of God in the world and more of the world in God; being sent out to men by him, and driven back to him by their hunger for redemption and love; refusing to give prayer alone when they need bread, but just as firmly refusing to give bread alone when they need prayer;* grieving that the world has so completely forsaken God and that he has seemingly forsaken it; devising a form of prayer that doesn't cut us off from the world, and a kind of work that won't estrange us from God.

---

*It'd be naive to imagine that modern man suffers only from physical hunger and sexual repressions. Above all, we're starved and repressed in regard to faith, hope, true love and prayer. Although these are the food, the natural climate, the fundamental respiration of the human soul, we ceaselessly fight them; and our ignorant rejection of them leaves most of us stunted, maimed and asphyxiated. Thus Paul, charging full of zeal and hate down the road to Damascus, learned—in a revelation that was a shock of psychoanalysis—that he was only repressing and smothering a voice inside him that had long been moaning, "Saul, Saul, why are you persecuting me?"

63

All this is an endless and agonizing task, but an essential one for our time. We must invent the spirituality of the age as we live out its problem: to be fully human, to remain solidary with all men and even the entire cosmos, and, at the same time, be fully open, offered and given up to God.

The great Christians of our era—Saint Thérèse of the Child Jesus, Maurice Blondel, Charles de Foucauld, Teilhard de Chardin—have all faced and wrestled with this problem. Both a contemplative and now the official patroness of the missions, Saint Thérèse, by reacting against false concepts of reparation and deliberate suffering, led French Carmelites back to their authentic vocation of human and divine love. Her spirit shines through in this axiom: "On earth, fraternal charity is everything; and we love God only insofar as we practice it." Teilhard de Chardin dreamed of a modern-day Francis of Assisi or Ignatius who'd come and teach us the new style of Christian life we need—at once, more involved in the world and more detached from it. Starting as a hermit and then becoming a "universal little brother," Charles de Foucauld gave up the Mass and the Real Presence, which literally possessed him, so that he might be closer to his Tuareg brothers. In the process, his triad, "To love Jesus, imitate him, and keep him company," became "To love Jesus, imitate him, and be a savior with him." On another level, Blondel spent his whole life evolving a Christian philosophy. All these great hearts expressed and probed the needs of our epoch.

The strongest proof of love we can offer anyone

is to show him a likeness of himself in which he can recognize and accept himself. What artists never tire of creating for their contemporaries, or lovers for their beloved, and teachers for their pupils, is precisely what contemplatives should discover for each era so that everyone who doesn't pray, or thinks he doesn't know how, may with amazement hear himself pray in their prayer.

In many respects, our liturgy, our patterns of prayer, our monasteries and churches are as ill-suited to actual needs as a thirteenth-century fresco in an exhibit of abstract art. When they were fashioned, they voiced and satisfied the desires of that time; but today, very few of us can recognize our prayer in theirs. Civilization, art and religion consist of a certain number of visions in which every man can recognize and understand himself, and without which a whole race dies.

It's happening to us. We're dying. We don't pray any more, and we don't know how to. The Church's aristocratic liturgy and its rigid, overrefined structures of worship no longer train the Christian people in the art of prayer. From this viewpoint, all too many have reverted to a sort of barbarism. Worse yet, just as exaggerated deism and clericalism paved the way for modern atheism, emphasis on form has bred impatience with prayer and hostility toward it. Consequently, scores of militant Catholics and even young priests consider prayer as an escape, a web of illusions and lies, a waste of time, an outlet for spiritual egoism, an orgy of religious sentiment and a disguise for narcissism.

All these deviations stem from ignorance of true prayer and, unfortunately, are found in many a "pious soul." If the people who love this world and love God, too, resolved to pray with both loves in their heart, they'd develop a prayer that would silence all objections. Reading René Voillaume's *In the Midst of Men* or Teilhard de Chardin's *The Divine Milieu* has made some of us sense what the spirituality of our age could be. They've discovered that they fit and want and need this kind of prayer—a prayer that doesn't oblige them to renounce a particle of what's most real to them: respect for their work and solidarity with their brothers.

We can't be Christians unless we're passionately in love with the world; unless we're like the Father, who so loved the world that he sent his Son into it to save it. We can't be Christians unless we're enthusiastic about our era, bound up with its destiny, responsible for its salvation, and engaged in vital communion with it, with all that's noble and beautiful in it, and with everything it suffers and achieves. Ours is a great age, one that grasps the tragedy of our human condition. It doesn't believe or, rather, doesn't know what or whom to believe in; but it suffers from its nonbelief—and that's a beginning of faith. It also suffers from its inability to hope—and that's a form of hope; just as suffering from unlove, from incapacity to love, is already a step toward love, a lowly and violent way of loving. Compared to this, the indifference and frivolity of some periods are odious.

The problem we're studying is part of an age-old debate on action versus contemplation. In our day, the

Dictionnaire de spiritualité still says, "Experience often proved that activity in the world dispersed the soul, attached the heart to this earth and fostered self-love, whereas the surest way to live with God was to contemplate him in the desert."

Saint Ignatius of Loyola, on the contrary, holds that, out of a hundred persons who engage in lengthy prayer and protracted mortification, the majority usually reap undesirable results—especially rigorism in their way of judging. Romano Guardini, in his *Prayer in Practice,* insists that prayer can't shun "active participation in life" without becoming emasculated. The receptive (or female) element in prayer is essential, but it degenerates if isolated from the active (or male) element called work. So-called "pure" prayer is "a passive affair" that soon languishes and faints. To remedy "the disturbance of balance," it must set out to achieve what it requests. The Our Father isn't only a prayer but a program of action. The kingdom of God has to be constructed, and, since his plan unfolds according to men and circumstances, we must find ways to actualize it daily under the inspiration of grace and prayer. "Christian prayer," Guardini writes, "has to a large extent lost contact with life as it now is. . . . The future of Christian life depends, among other things, on whether prayer can establish an active link with life as it is and with the stream of history."[1]

But that's enough quoting. We'll never be able

[1] Romano Guardini, *Prayer in Practice,* translated by Prince Leopold of Lowenstein-Wertheim (New York: Image Books, 1963), p. 121.

to clarify this question until we drop the word and the idea of *contemplation,* which is Greek, unevangelical ("No one has ever seen God"[2]), and most inadequate. Christianity is much more than contemplation: it's participation. God isn't only the object, the goal, the immobile end of our quest; he's at the beginning of it, as the cause, the mover, the movement and the grace. Not only is he loved, but he himself loves in us—loves far more than he is loved, because we resist so many of his inspirations.

Contemplation evokes a pseudo religion in which we're the ones who do things for God and draw near him, whereas in the true religion, he's the one who does great things with the poverty of his servants. Prayer is a grace; it's infused and it comes from God, who is the beginning, the means and the end of it. When we pray, we needn't think we're performing the feat of coming to contemplate God. Rather than sighs of effort or satisfaction, we should heave cries of joy; for God's already at work shaping us, and he has already won the incredible victory of persuading us to pray. Believe me, we'd never do it of ourselves. In my own case, for example, it's always on the way to church or chapel that I become most eager to help, that I suddenly remember a job I've left unfinished, a letter I haven't answered, a favor that seemed impossible before, and a hundred pretexts to postpone, trim or fritter away the time allotted to prayer.

God is the one who prays and loves in us.[3] Infi-

---

[2] See 1 Jn. 4, 12 (and note *e* in *The Jerusalem Bible*).
[3] See Rom. 8, 26.

nitely better than we are, he associates us with his prayer, with his love and the cultus he renders himself, with the murmur of admiration, gratitude and reverence that unceasingly rises from the heart of the Son toward the Father. Nothing less than this notion of participation can resolve the problem of prayer and action. God loves in us, through activity as well as prayer; God loves himself in us, and others through us; God becomes alive in us and, because he's alive, propels us toward all men. Consequently, there's no dichotomy between prayer and action. Prayer is the time God uses to love and reanimate himself in us, and activity is the normal expression of this love. How could we know and love a God who "goes on working"[4] and yet not be impelled to act?

Someone will surely object, "What about the symbolism of the Martha and Mary episode?" All I can say is that I don't understand how anything so clear could be misinterpreted so often and so completely. It's false and outrageous to make Martha the model of the active life. She wasn't active at all: she was restless.

When our Lord speaks, there's just one thing to *do,* and that's to listen. A genuinely active person, attentive and close to reality, would have soaked up his every sentence, since there's nothing more operative than the word of God. But Martha wasn't content with that. Christ's inner action didn't interest her enough to make her sit still and listen; driven by her nerves, she had to go let off steam among her pots and pans. The

[4] Jn. 5, 17.

Lord was too demanding and required such close attention that she went to rest in the kitchen, where it was
much less tiresome. And, to top it all, she couldn't
stand seeing her sister do what she herself was incapa-
ble of, so she came back and interrupted the Lord to
see whether he couldn't get Mary to putter around with
the dishes, too.

But Mary was no idle sob sister, no pious jelly-
fish. When, after Lazarus' death, Martha announced,
"The Master is here and wants to see you" (another
way to agitate her!), Mary got up "quickly," says Saint
John, and went to him.[5] In particular, what we invariably forget in discussing Mary is the mission our risen
Lord gave her. Although she tried to prolong her
adoration—her contemplation—unduly, he wouldn't let
her cling to his feet but ordered, "Go and find my
brothers."[6] Granted that he first made himself known,
patiently and tenderly, still he didn't let her coo very
long once she had really rediscovered him. Modeling
her on his own heart, he sent her out to others. And she
went.

Despite a long-standing belief partly shared by
Saint Thomas among others, the Gospels don't con-
demn action, work or foresight, but only anxiety.
There's no such thing as "the duty of improvidence";
on the contrary, we're bound in conscience to be sensible and prudent and, therefore, provident—but without
becoming apprehensive. Four times in nine verses of

[5] Jn. 11, 28-29.
[6] Jn. 20, 17 (and note g).

Saint Matthew we're told not to worry,[7] and that's all Martha was chided for: "Martha, Martha, you worry and fret about so many things . . . ."[8] Now, disquiet, tension and anxiety, far from accomplishing anything, prevent us from acting. Whereas confidence liberates us, worry absorbs and paralyzes us. Christ defines and advocates the conditions that are indispensable to real action as well as real prayer; he censures only what hampers them both. In a nutshell, we must pray and work with faith.

Yet somehow we've failed to see that "the one thing needed," "the better part" that Mary chose, wasn't the false beatitude "Happy the womb that bore you and the breasts you sucked" but the true one that described Jesus' mother: "Still happier those who hear the word of God and keep it!"[9]

Why must we adore God and consecrate to his worship time that's specially set aside, gratuitously given and seemingly lost to all else? Because, short of that, God can't be God for us. He needs time; he wants part of our time. As we said before, he demands only what modern servants demand—consideration. But he doesn't get it. He wishes to be considered in both senses of the word, which implies respect and attention: he wants us to consider him, he wants us to take time to consider him.

[7] See Mt. 6, 25.28.31 and 34.
[8] Lk. 10, 41.
[9] Lk. 11, 27-18.

God occupies in our esteem the same place he occupies in our schedule. We find time for everything we deem important. No matter how busy we are, we never leave the house without grooming ourselves, or work all day without eating and drinking; very few of us skip the morning paper; we rest and even indulge in occasional entertainment; we may be late with our chores, but the minute a friend asks to see us, we drop everything and welcome him. In short, we make time for whatever seems worthwhile; and if we don't make time for God, it's because we don't think he rates it.

In practice, no time for prayer means no faith in God. Oh, we'll yearn and sigh and complain that we haven't the leisure to pray—all the more so, perhaps, the less we actually do pray (like the philanderer who admires his wife more than ever). But unless we set aside periods for prayer, we'll be virtual atheists—atheists who aspire after the religious life and intend to pray if ever we have a chance.

We must give God time to speak, and ourselves time to listen. Since he requires that, we need enough patience to wait till we've learned how to listen to him. When we begin to pray and examine our life, it looks like a jungle so dense we can't see or reach God any more. The oppressive atmosphere drags us to the ground, where our hands and feet are inextricably caught in a tangled undergrowth of self-love, weariness, heartache, disgust and resentment. We'll never break loose, humanly speaking, never be able to move ahead. But if we continue to pray, if we nail our body to the pew and our eyes on God, if we persevere in exposing our interior swamp to the rays of the divine Sun, then, little by little right there before us, God becomes real, God becomes alive and close, God becomes tender and wise and just and powerful and active, God becomes God. Meanwhile, imperceptibly, the steaming mist has begun to lift and the brush that blocked our path recedes at a flick of the wrist. It's true that prayer moves mountains. We can bear ourselves again, and life has become livable—all because God has regained his place: the first; and we've resumed ours: the second.

But it takes a good while for God to become God in us once more, to regain the throne we keep usurping. The whole Christian life consists in participating in Christ's death and resurrection. At baptism we died: we were drowned and buried in the waters of death; then we emerged entirely new, streaming with lustral water, in the splendor of a new creation, like clay which the potter has drenched to shape it anew. (The freshness of the world when the waters first rushed forth! The amazement of Noah when he saw the first green bough of the first spring on this renovated earth! The illumination of John the Baptist when the New Adam stood beside the waters of the Jordan! The conversion of the world when the apostles came out filled with the Holy Spirit!)

Each confession is a death and a resurrection. What an opportunity: we can get rid of ourselves, disappear, die! All we have to do is step into a confessional. There we die to our desires—to the poor, dismal, leaden desires called sin; and there we resurrect to God's will, which is love, hope, tenderness, faith, and patience with ourselves and others. Similarly, the Mass makes us share in Christ's death to self and his own will, and resurrect to the Father's.

But prayer, also—prayer above all—is when we must die to self and resurrect to God. It's when he becomes incarnate in our lives. To pray is to put ourselves at his disposal so that, at last, he can achieve in us what he has always wanted and what we've never given him time or opportunity for. Prayer detaches us from what we feel and attaches us to what we believe: the truth that we're God's sons and daughters.

I don't know of any prayer that's "short but good." Prayer has too much to accomplish in us to do it fast. We always start by asking for the wrong thing or the right thing in the wrong way; we approach prayer full of ourselves, whereas God wants to fill us with himself. So he makes us wait till we're ready to receive, not some grace that'll enable us to do without him, but the total gift of himself. He lets us die in a slow prayer, like Lazarus, so that he can make us live with his own life. But how could we ever carry a message of resurrection unless we died first? How could we go out to others unless we took the time and the trouble to die?*

*This is the main reason why the sacraments are so often inefficacious. Lest they seem like magical rites, they should be surrounded with prayers and ceremonies that dispose us to receive the grace they communicate. Instead, we've so shortened them and so fogged them with unintelligible language and ritual that they can't do this any longer. (For instance, the reconciliation of public sinners once took forty days, but

Let's not be like musicians who are so preoc-
cupied and enthusiastic about the concert that they
don't even bother to tune their instruments. Too expan-
sive and outgoing, they're overly interested in the en-
semble and imagine they're pleasing everyone while
playing hopelessly off pitch. As for us, we're so haunted
by the idea of saving the world that we pay attention to
everyone but hesitate to pause a minute and think of
God. We respect others and are careful to treat them
like persons; we strive to humanize our dealings because we're convinced that the poorest and lowliest

---

we get through confession in two minutes; the catechumenate
used to last three years, but now baptism is over in fifteen
minutes; most of our Masses have been demoted to "low";
and so on.)

The average Christian sees the sacraments as pills or
religion capsules, as decorations or good-conduct medals; but
he isn't willing to die in them and doesn't yearn to resurrect in
them. He utilizes priests but won't listen to them, because
he's sure he grasps religion better than they and, accordingly,
takes some and leaves some. By and large, the faithful consider the sacraments a solemnity to enhance their celebrations
and a heaven-insurance to be added to their life-, fire-, or ac-
cident-insurance. They protect themselves from God but refuse to "lose" their life. Quite the contrary: they avail themselves of the clergy to safeguard that life all the more surely,
and they have no desire to resurrect, to know a higher life, to
change and become Another.

As a result, there's a fundamental contradiction between the proper effect of the sacrament and the dispositions
they bring to it. All is made barren. Now, according to Saint
Paul, there's only one sin: to be and to remain one's "old
self"; and only one Christian condition: not being Jew or

man on earth counts and must be thought of as a
unique being. Well, God is a person, too. He's poor,
rejected and forsaken. "Look, I am standing at the
door, knocking."[10] He tries to exist in our eyes and
count in our lives. All he asks is a little consideration;
and we'll never learn really to consider others "in his
name" unless we take the trouble to consider him in
himself and let him teach us how.

We often say our work is a prayer. I hope it is: I
hope our faith and love and reverence sharply distin-
guish it from the work of unbelievers or, more exactly,
indifferentists. But if we believe in God and if we love
him, how can we neglect to stop once in a while and tell
him so? The gratuitous is what we need most in life. If
our existence is purely functional, it's subhuman; if we
don't pause to look and admire, to love, to laugh and
sing, we're robots. We work for our wife and children,
also, and our fatigue is proof that we love them. But is
that enough for us? Don't we ever stop to tell them so?

With legitimate pride, modern Christians repeat,
"God needs men; he has chosen to need us!" Yet rare

_____

Greek, slave or free, male or female, but simply being "a new
creature."

It's almost pointless to administer the sacraments to
people who don't pray and don't want to, who refuse to die,
and wish only to remain themselves in spite of everything.
Clearly, we'd have to celebrate the sacraments in such an authentic, realistic and telling way that no one could take part
in them without experiencing a death and a resurrection.

[10] Rev. 3, 20.

are those who explain why and how much man needs God. Believers and unbelievers alike proclaim that respect for human dignity is the basis of our civilization and that we consider man sacred. Still, we should all add (if only because we know ourselves) how weak, variable and urgent this sacralizing is. There's nothing to fear: such an admission can only reinforce our efforts. God isn't selfish; he won't monopolize us and hinder our "apostolate." After all, to be an apostle is to be sent out, to come from him—on his part.

God is the one who sends us out to our brothers; he loves them much more than we do; and his is the love we must announce to them—*before* ours. "All others who have come before me are thieves and brigands . . . [who have come] only to steal and kill and destroy."[11] We protest, "What do you mean I'm a thief and a brigand? I'm helping my fellow men!" No, what we secretly want is to assert ourselves and dominate them, and our apostolate serves as an impressive pretext. Since we can't bear God or ourselves, we take it out on others; we make the apostolate a safety valve, an escape. We pretend that others need us, when the truth is that we love to feel needed. Instead of anchoring others in God, we merely anchor ourselves to them— like rowboats huddled together, but without a dock. Such are the vicious circles of the apostolate. "Oh, no, I'm dedicated to the truth. That's what I seek and that's what I speak." The trouble is, we love our own truth, the one we've discovered, the one that makes us special. If we heard it from someone else, we wouldn't

[11] See Jn. 10, 8.10.

prize it at all but attempt rather to disprove it. "I want to save So-and-So, and I'm willing to sacrifice myself and die for his salvation. Don't tell me I'm not disinterested!" Of course, we are—provided we're the saviors. But if somebody else is, do we still rejoice and thank God?

We can't always be giving: we have to receive as well. If we haven't received from God what we give to others, our activity will drain us and force us to recover in our apostolate the very strength we expend on it. We'll reimburse ourselves with the paltry gratifications of self-love or tyranny, of caprice, ill temper, bossiness or sentimentality. We'll be like a tired old draft horse that leans on the wagon shafts, supporting himself on what he's pulling: half propped up this way, he has only to jog along and let his burden sustain him till they both collapse.

Only if we've met God can we meet others in his name. Only if we're happy near him can we go out to our neighbor. It'd be preposterous to run up and down evangelizing men because we can't endure staying close to God any more, and recruit adorers for him because he bores us so much that we can't stand his presence and have to flee. We can't safely go forth till we'd rather stay behind. It was when Mary of Magdala wanted to clasp his feet that Jesus said, "Go and find my brothers."

Even if we're extraordinary and filled with wonderful qualities, we needn't think we're helping others by telling them they should imitate us. Everyone is dif-

ferent, and we can't give anybody what's peculiar to us.
No doubt, they'll be dazzled for a moment, and flat-
tered; but they'll soon learn that what's true for us isn't
true for them, and that what's good for us isn't neces-
sarily good for them, and that what's easy for us is
downright impossible for them.

Nothing that is specifically ours can be handed
on. God alone is communicable. The only thing we can
bear witness to is what he has accomplished in us; the
only comforting and saving message we can proclaim
concerns, not our superbly endowed character, but the
marvels he has achieved in the poverty of his servants.
"Speak but the word, and my soul will be healed."

I don't care if we're strong and courageous,
bursting with health and vitality, naturally pure and
generous. But if we're weaklings whom God strength-
ens, sensualists whom he purifies and contents, worry-
warts he soothes, cowards he reassures, misers liberated
from their possessions, or grudge-bearers who've
learned to forgive—then our story can interest others,
our message can hit home; and since all men share in
our wretchedness, they can all hope for the same cure.

We can transmit only what we've received from
Christ. The only meaningful testimony we can bear him
is that he has done in us precisely what we could never
do. It takes a dead man to bear tidings of resurrection.
The Good News, the Gospel we must announce to the
world, is that we can fall sick and get well, stumble and
stand up once more, be sinners and find ourselves not
only forgiven but loved and coddled and favored—in a

word, die and live again. God alone is ready to help us; he alone is beneficent and indispensable.

We're so weak that we need all of God's power in us just to stay on our feet; so impure that we need God himself to be pure in us. We're so greedy that it takes all his riches to detach us from our baubles; so cold and dry that it takes every spark of his love, enkindled in our hearts, just to cherish, as we should and as they need, those who are closest to us, those to whom we've promised and to whom we owe most love.

Ours won't be a living religion, adult and communicable, till we can say to our parents, teachers and pastors what the crowd told the Samaritan woman after they had spent two days—enough time for a weekend retreat—with Christ: "Now we no longer believe because of what you told us; we have heard him ourselves and we know that he really is the saviour of the world."[12] Do we believe in God—or in those who've spoken to us about him? Only if he himself has spoken to us, only if we've frequented him ourselves, only if he has saved us personally can we tell the world about salvation and the love of God.

And yet, though I believe that prayer alone can dispel the illusions of activity, I believe just as firmly that activity alone—loving, fraternal activity—can dispel the illusions of prayer.

For there's nothing more dangerous than reli-

[12] Jn. 4, 42.

gious sentiment; and, unfortunately, prayer cultivates
it. It's a frightful, devouring passion that begets fanati-
cism, holy wars, cruelty and madness, the cult of Moloch and the extermination of women and children.
Next to it, the other passions seem innocent. People
have committed the worst atrocities and shown themselves most heartless, most merciless and most inhu-
man in the name of the very God who became man.
Few things are so ruthless as the zeal of certain apostles
—like Saul, "breathing threats to slaughter the Lord's
disciples" and going to the high priest "for let-
ters . . . that would authorize him to arrest . . . any
followers of the Way."[13] Few things are so stony as
the heart of certain Christians who are addicted to piety
—like the Corinthians who were warned by Saint Paul
that the meetings they held to celebrate the Lord's Supper did them "more harm than good."[14]

There's one class of people Christ couldn't abide
and never won over: the Pharisees, who can best be
described as devout but grimly religious souls. Pharisees are persons whose piety hardens and sours them.
They're so set on being divine that they become in-
human. Once they've scrupulously squared their account
with God, they feel free to juggle their accounts with
the neighbor, as if being on good terms with the Father
in heaven allowed them to be on bad terms with the man
next door. But Christ has taught us that we stand in the
same relationship to God as to our fellow men and that
we're no closer to him than we are to them. Pharisees

[13] Acts 9, 1-2.
[14] 1 Cor. 11, 17.

would be better if they weren't so religious. For they imagine ritual dispenses them from truth, and Communion from sharing; they carry their gifts to the altar but remain aloof and indifferent to their brother; they profess to love God, whom they don't see, and thus reassure themselves about not loving their neighbor, whom they do see—and see only too much.

For many, religion is "so comforting": God solaces us for not loving others, and we take refuge in him all the more as we can't get along with anyone. But the Spirit of Consolation has only one way of consoling us: he sends us back to our fellow men, determined to restore harmony and start loving all over again. True contemplatives become active and go out to mankind, whereas false contemplatives add a new stone to their "enclosure" every day. The word *Pharisee* means "separated," "removed." Yet Christ prayed, "I am not asking you to remove them from the world, but to protect them from evil."[15]

We shouldn't turn to prayer as to an artificial paradise that nurtures sentimentality, rigorism or complacence. Unfortunately, many a prayer is withdrawal more than receptiveness, introspection more than communion, self-absorption more than attention to the Other. How many people ever think of praying the Credo, for instance? "But that's not really a prayer," they object; "it doesn't say a thing about us!" No, all it talks about is God and the glorious things he does in his lowly servants. It's a sort of Magnificat, and for that

[15] Jn. 17, 15.

reason we rarely say it on our own. The Our Father and
the Hail Mary are pretty interesting, though, because
the second part of them mentions us and affords us a
chance to think of ourselves with tender warmth. Some
of us even add a word: "Pray for us *poor* sinners now
and at the hour of our death," as if examining with pity
and satisfaction the "poor little sinners we are." The
Credo's magnificent objectivity will rescue us from this
emotional quicksand.

Against the danger of illusion and sentimentality, we must constantly affirm the religion of the
God-Man, of theandrism, of the Incarnation. Even in
the Old Testament, the ultimate task of the prophets
was to link religious feeling—the sense of sacredness—
with social morality and justice. They inveighed against
ritual divorced from brotherhood: "Let your hearts be
broken, not your garments torn."[16] "Is not this the sort
of fast that pleases me . . . to break unjust fet-
ters . . . to let the oppressed go free . . . to share
your bread with the hungry, and shelter the homeless
poor, to clothe the man you see to be naked and not
turn from your own kin?"[17] "Put no trust in delusive
words like these: This is the sanctuary of Yahweh. . . . But if you do amend your behaviour and
your actions . . . then here in this place I will stay
with you."[18] "What are your endless sacrifices to me?
says Yahweh. I am sick of holocausts and rams and the
fat of calves. The blood of bulls and of goats revolts

[16] Joel 2, 13.
[17] Is. 58, 6-7.
[18] Jer. 7, 4-7.

me. . . . I cannot endure festival and solemnity. Your New Moons and your pilgrimages I hate with all my soul."[19] "Let me have no more of the din of your chanting, no more of your strumming on harps. But let justice flow like water, and integrity like an unfailing stream."[20]

If they were writing now, they'd say, "Your Masses offend me, your Communions are lies, your assemblies set you apart and you use the sacraments like magic formulas." For Jesus, by his Incarnation as well as his new commandment, has indivisibly united love of man and love of God. Although the Old Testament enjoined us to love our neighbor as ourselves, we call Christ's commandment new since he made it "the same" as the first and equal to it, since he actually turned the second commandment into the first by becoming man so that man could become God. God is no longer in his heaven, and we shouldn't wait for him to appear in triumph on a bank of clouds. He's right here, right now—eaten in the bread, swallowed in the wine, despised in the most insignificant of men, and so closely yoked to us that we invariably overlook him when searching for him.

Yet we mustn't search for him, but simply accept his word. We mustn't invent him, but—which is already hard enough—accept him as he presents himself and as he rubs elbows with us. Jesus has sacralized man and desacralized everything else—the Sabbath, the

[19] Is. 1, 11-14.
[20] Amos 5, 23-24.

Temple, fasting, priests and Levites (they're vastly inferior to a charitable heretic unless their devotion flowers into devotedness) and cultus itself. "If you are bringing your offering to the altar and there remember that your brother has something against you, leave your offering there before the altar, go and be reconciled with your brother first, and then come back and present your offering."[21] "What I want is mercy, not sacrifice."[22] Only one thing defiles us: refusing to love. Ritual without charity damns a man; conversely, charity—even without ritual—saves him,[23] but like a savage who can't name or know the God he reveres and serves.

Have you ever noticed that Saint John, whose Gospel is so sacramental, doesn't relate the institution of the Eucharist? I think that's because he relates the institution of another sacrament, of which the Eucharist is only the source and the sign: namely, the washing of the feet—brotherly love. His narrative opens with a sort of majestic prelude that's brusquely interrupted by a return to plainest reality: "It was before the festival of the Passover, and Jesus knew that the hour had come for him to pass from this world to the Father. He had always loved those who were his in the world, but now he showed how perfect his love was. They were at supper. . . . Jesus knew that the Father had put everything into his hands, and that he had come from God and was returning to God, and he got up from table, removed his outer garment and, taking a towel,

[21] Mt. 5, 23-24.
[22] Mt. 9, 13; 12, 7.
[23] See Mt. 7, 21-23; Lk. 13, 25-27; Mt. 25, 37-40.

wrapped it round his waist; he then poured water into a basin and began to wash the disciples' feet and to wipe them with the towel he was wearing." (Similarly, Saint Matthew begins to describe the last judgment in the style of the celestial, apocalyptic religion of a transcendent and awe-inspiring God, only to jolt us with the gripping realism of "I was hungry, I was thirsty."[24]) Like the Consecration at Mass, Saint John's account ends with a memorial: "I have given you an example so that you may copy what I have done to you."[25]

John wanted to tell us that we'd always have a sacrament close by, a means of communicating that'd never fail us, an object of worship that'd be with us everywhere—Christ, hidden and abased in our fellow man. Brotherly love is the only sacrament for which there are no substitutes. All the others can be replaced: the baptism of water by that of desire, Communion by longing, and confession by perfect contrition; but nothing will ever dispense us from loving our neighbor—and especially not "Lord, Lord!"

*　　*　　*

Clearly, there's no brotherhood without adoration or without Fatherhood; no apostolate unless we're sent out; no charity that isn't infused (prayer corresponds to this "infused" character of grace); and no Redemption without an Incarnation. Our supernatural fruitfulness, like Mary's, will depend on our receptivity.

[24] See Mt. 25, 31-46.
[25] Jn. 13, 1-15.

But, just as clearly, there's no such thing as adoration without brotherhood. Before the Blessed Sacrament exposed, we shouldn't limit our adoration to Christ but ask ourselves two questions that will allow us to broaden it.

First, "Who made this host?" We have to realize why our Lord chose to appear to us under the symbol and inside the substance of man's labor and fatigue. It's because he wanted to consecrate, to divinify and eternalize them. Therefore, let's not exalt the host so much that we dissociate it from our work.

And second, "Who's going to eat it?" The host is meant to be eaten far more than exposed and adored. Its whole purpose is to be chewed so that we can absorb it. Christ willed to become broken bread, to be shared and divided, in order "to gather together in unity the scattered children of God."[26] We can't let our adoration stop at the host but, rather, extend it to each and every man who'll eat Christ's body.

Our neighbor is a monstrance—sometimes just as unmanageable as the metal ones and full of the thorns suggested by those golden "rays." It's too easy to adore a host while disowning the people who receive it. We must understand that the Lord wanted us to recognize him under the drab and prosaic appearance of bread first, so that we'd learn to recognize him under another form, just as ordinary and nondescript—our neighbor.

[26] Jn. 11, 52.

We revere the body of Christ given us in Communion; but do we revere the body which we all form together, or do we sometimes tear it to pieces? We shake with horror when we hear of sacrilegious persons stealing hosts to inflict outrages and dagger wounds on them; but what do we think of people whose hostility, prejudice, selfishness or mere unconcern dismembers the true body of the living Christ? Which is worse: profaning the means or the end, the food or the person, the bread or the body?

At the last judgment, we won't be asked whether we've adored the Eucharist but whether we've loved our brothers as adoration should teach us to do. The Gospels amply illustrate how each act of adoration leads to brotherliness: everyone who saw and recognized the Lord, everyone who heard and understood him, was sent forth to others.

What did the Blessed Virgin do after the Annunciation—make a retreat, a day of recollection? No, a visitation, rather: she went to help Elizabeth with the housework. (If ever we have visions, we shouldn't linger over them but go help our wife do the dishes. It's an excellent way to check one's ecstasies.) Without sermonizing, she preached so well by silent example that Elizabeth was moved to prophecy and even her unborn child could sense her rapture. After the resurrection, Jesus favored Mary of Magdala with a glimpse of himself and, at the very same moment, with a mission to her brothers. The disciples from Emmaus recognized Christ in the breaking of the bread and immediately set out to share their joy with the Eleven.

In that tender dialogue between Christ and Peter after the miraculous catch of fish (almost like thanksgiving after Communion), Jesus asked him, "Simon, son of John, do you love me?" And as soon as Peter answered, "Lord, you know everything; you know I love you," Jesus entrusted the others to him: "Feed my sheep."[27] In other words, "Devote yourself to them, look after them."

At Pentecost, hardly had the apostles received the Holy Spirit when, without the space of a thanksgiving, they were thrust into the street to announce and share with the world the gift they had been given. And Paul himself, once he had made his retreat—three days without seeing, eating or drinking—was referred to a brother. He had to join the Church; and, since he was an impetuous and individualistic genius, the Lord just happened to direct him toward Ananias, whom some moderns would describe as a "formalistic, over-prudent, obstructive and timorous pastor." For Paul, there was no communion with the Lord except through his brother, who so inadequately and so prophetically represented God's Church—the body of Christ.

[27] Jn. 21, 17.

Truth in Prayer

Prayer is an experience of faith as well as an encounter, a relationship, with the living God. Quite naturally, then, we may ask why we pray, what happens when we do, and whether we meet someone there or simply fool ourselves. To answer these questions, we'll study the interconnections between prayer, our life, our activity, our suffering and our love.

Prayer is a superexcellent place to meet the Lord. Unless we pray, we don't know him or what he's like and we can't be converted.

I'm convinced that there's nothing more sincere than the prayer of an unbeliever—and goodness knows we're all unbelievers in whole broad areas of our existence. Just what does that matchless sincerity consist in? Very simply: seeking. All I can say to an infidel, to myself or to you, is this: "You're looking for the truth, for a meaning to your life. Well, so am I; I'm forever looking and—take my word for it—finding more and more all the time. Whenever I discover something, I tell myself I haven't understood a thing so far and I visualize all that's yet to be learned. Faith isn't a downy pillow to rest our head on, but a vehement drive to invent, to create. Amazing how the Gospel is always new! I haven't understood a word of it yet, so I'll have to keep reading it over and over. You see, I'm like you— an unbeliever, always searching. It's inconceivable what I'm searching for and what I'm discovering, too.

"But, tell me, do you think truth is some*thing* or some*one*? I say it's some*one*. The way I interpet my experience, truth has entered my life like a person, and I've ascertained that it really is. God is someone; he's a person. This mad and terrifying demiurge of creation has shown himself meek and humble of heart. He's a person; he's a revelation.

"You, a priori, can't say one way or the other. But if you want to investigate the matter thoroughly, honestly and scientifically, you've got to examine both hypotheses. If truth is a thing, I understand your desire to conquer it by means of arguments and demonstrations, research and scholarship, debates and discussions. I can understand your spirit of acquisition and ownership. On the other hand, if truth is someone, if it's a person, you must go out to meet it in an entirely different frame of mind—an attitude of respectful attention, of openness and receptivity. To be sufficiently disponible and poor at heart, you've got to pray; otherwise, granting that truth is a person, you'll never be able to embrace it."

How can we get to know the people around us? There are several ways. For one, we can stretch them out on a table and dissect them. For another, we can submit them to psychological tests and gather a series of facts about them. But the surest method is twofold: first, for us to look at them, to remain silent and so interiorize ourselves that we sense a rapport with what's most interior in them; and, secondly, for them to trust us and come and speak to us. It's a mutual giving.

And that's what prayer is—a chance for God to utter himself. To welcome someone, though, we have to open up; to receive a gift, we have to give ourselves.

At twenty-five, Julien Green was caught in a whirlwind of debauchery. (A witless spiritual director had told him, "Unless you enter a monastery, I fear for your salvation!" After that, of course, Green let go completely. Why not? He didn't want to become a monk, the "world" was the vestibule to hell, and he most probably couldn't save his soul anyway. So, full speed ahead.) Driven on by the madness of the flesh and convinced he'd never be able to free himself again, he wrote in his diary: "I asked that a hand be extended to me." That's the prayer of the poor. He treated God like a person and was converted. Here's a point worth pondering: to realize that a hand has been held out to us, we must hold ours out also; to touch the hand that has been proffered, we must proffer ours. Short of that, we absolutely can't know. I say "know," not "obtain," because it has already been done: God's hand has already been tendered to us. Our prayer isn't what changes him. But we have to reach out if we're to notice that a hand is stretched out to us.

After her conversion, Edith Stein said, "For years, the thirst for truth was my only prayer." What a beautiful prayer! And what a heroic one—for some, at least—if truth turns out to be a person! We must seek the truth and accept it, even if it's a person, even if it demands everything of us. Unless an unbeliever prays in this spirit, there's no use continuing, for he's arbitrarily ruling out a possibility and limiting himself to half the field of investigation.

Still, we must be careful how we view prayer. Just as a great deal of paganism, godlessness and natural religion have reappeared under the cloak of Christianity, so have they infiltrated prayer. There's a kind of prayer that's pagan and another that's Christian, and they're worlds apart.

Though the apostles had prayed much and long, Christ equivalently told them, at the Last Supper, that they had never prayed right and didn't know how. "Until now you have not asked for anything in my name. Ask and you will receive, and so your joy will be complete."[1] They must have been jolted, just as we are when we stop to examine our prayer life. "What, all those hours of adoration down the drain? Who ever heard of such a thing? He ought to appreciate our contemplative repose a little more!" Yet Christ says we've been praying the wrong way and teaches us what to do.

Let's explore the nature of Christian prayer somewhat. Happily (though, unhappily, it keeps recurring), we've long since outgrown the notion that prayer is supposed to change God, making a distracted God attentive, telling a poorly informed God what's needed, bringing a slightly cold God up to the right temperature, and shaking him well before using.

Even so, all our prayers follow that tack instinc-

[1] Jn. 16, 24.

tively. We always start the wrong way. Take a prayer at random, like "Pour your grace into our hearts, O Lord. . . ." Come, now, don't we believe he does that already? Our every prayer should be worded positively: "Lord, since you pour your grace into our hearts, we want to become conscious of it and open ourselves to its influence." As if we were out to change God, we always address him in the imperative mood. It'd be scandalous if we knew what we were doing; but, as we never think while we pray or notice how we pray, we swallow it all very easily. There's no other way to explain how we can constantly advise and direct God: "Lord, do this and do that. And, above all, don't forget us, for, at your age, you very well may!" Once we stop to think, though, nothing gets by; there isn't a prayer that doesn't pose some question.

The only person who must change in prayer is self. The very idea of praying comes, not from us, but from God, who's already at work in us and has led us to church. Provided we don't leave right away as we're tempted to do, but settle down and force ourselves to wait and listen, he may have time to tell us what he wants to say. We're not God; he is. We're not good; he is. We don't desire him; he desires us. Accordingly, praying is putting ourselves at God's disposal so that he can finally carry out his plans for us; it's preparing ourselves gradually to receive what grace alone inspires us to ask for.

What's the new prayer Christ taught his apostles? Praying in his name, in the name of the Son. And what does that mean? Not merely mouthing a formula but earnestly praying in a filial state of mind, under the impulsion of the Holy Spirit, who cries "Father" in our hearts. To pray, then, is to move from one level to another. Normally, we're the ones who think and act and will; but the moment we start to pray, we should let the Spirit lift us to the level of our adoption as sons.[2]

This takes time and docility. For Christ, it took a whole night—a whole night repeating one petition of the Our Father: "May your will be done." Yet we rush through the entire Our Father in a single breath. At that speed, of course, we're saying absolutely nothing. We must take it at God's pace: one long night for one short petition. . . .

If we try this, we'll never finish the prayer. Most likely, we won't get past the word *Father;* for once we've begun to fathom the meaning of it, once we've experienced the truth of it, what more is there to say? Faith should always be experienced like that, not just clung to because someone handed it down. When we recite the Credo, for instance, we mustn't on any account disbelieve but struggle to believe positively—that is, put meaning into it and experience the truth of it.

To sum up this first point, praying enables us to hear God as he begs that we open up to him, transforming our prayer till it becomes an expression of faith and surrender into his hands.

But enough about prayer for ourselves, which,

[2] Rom. 8, 15.

basically, is quite clear. Now let's discuss prayer for our brothers, which constitutes a crucial problem, a shameful lie, a canker in Christianity. From the moment someone says, "I'll pray for you," we can be sure he won't strain a muscle or lift a finger for us, since he feels excused from doing anything. After all, he's going to pray for us! Such promises make us shudder, for they mean that ours is a hopeless case and that he washes his hands of it. Too often, prayer is an alibi.

Take grace before meals. It used to run "Bless us, O Lord, and these your gifts. . . ." Now we add, "Bless those who have prepared our food" and, having granted them a passing nod, we're content. Or perhaps we even say, ". . . and give bread to those who have none," after which we settle down to a hearty meal and let God worry about the rest of humanity. (Every man for himself, you know, and God for all. . . .) That kind of prayer is the easy way out, shockingly cynical. Authentic prayer would have us insist, "Make us find bread for those who don't have any," because God has no one but us to do the very things we ask him for.

There's something to meditate on: God has no one but us to do the very things we ask him for. He established the Church—a living presence among men— to answer the same prayers it makes to God.

When we plead, "Give us this day our daily bread," we needn't imagine he's going to bake little buns and send them down to us from heaven. We've lost touch with reality if we think he's going to turn stones into bagels, multiply loaves and make rolls rain down on the little Chinese children just because we mumble, "Give us this day our daily bread." Bluntly, we're knee-deep in pious deception.

Any sincere prayer compels us to share what we have. There's only one way for God to distribute bread to those who lack it, and that's for us to give them ours. There's only one chance for underdeveloped nations to have bread, and that's for the West—which happens to be the Christian West—to help them grow it. God's honor depends on us.

It's up to us to preserve ourselves and the world from evil by means of inventions, teaching and services, technology, science and engineering. Prayer is nothing but scandalous flimflam if we use it to shift our responsibilities onto God. This is a mentality our contemporaries detest, and they refuse to pray if it seems to mean saddling him with the tasks they themselves ought to be doing.

God isn't a limit set on man. We can't just sit back and say, "What we don't understand, he'll reveal to us; and what we can't do, he'll do in our stead"—unless, of course, ours is the kind of God who loses ground as we gain and retreats as we advance, unless we fear that each discovery diminishes the number of miracles to be sought, and unless we think human progress will eventually obviate the need for him. What a small view of God!

When I was newly ordained, people used to come for the blessing in honor of Saint Apollonia against toothache. Thank heavens, they don't anymore. Instead, they brush their teeth and have regular checkups. The same with Saint Roch for hydrophobia: they prudently take an antirabic vaccine. Perhaps we still pray for rain or sunshine, but we won't any longer once we've learned how to control the weather—as we certainly will, what with satellites and all. Does that mean God will fade out of the picture even more? Quite the contrary. It simply means that we'll have devised a way of doing what God fitted us to do for ourselves.

Somewhere along the line, we've developed the notion that, with prayer, we have a sort of checking account in heaven and that God transfers our funds for us: we simply tell him what we want, and he does the work. Still, there's nothing purely spiritual in the Church—nothing. The Church isn't in the material order, but it isn't in the ideal, either; it's in the sacramental order, where there's always a sensible sign. In fact, the Church itself is a sacrament, a sensible sign of God's presence, of his word, and of his love in the world. Because of the Church's charity, men can believe in God's; because the Church gives bread, they can trust that he will.

Whether we care to or not, we must face the fact that our mode of acting on others can't be solely spiritual. Every time we pray for someone else, we should be driven to do something for him. That's the first and authentic effect of all such prayer. And once we see things in this perspective, we discover what thoughtless Christians can't understand: that there's always something we can do. Whenever I say this, half of my listeners protest, "But, Father, you must admit there are some people you just can't help." The latest objection is "What about Vietnam?" Our conception of prayer has so anesthetized us that we're convinced there's nothing to be done there. Yet have we taken part in demonstrations against further bombings? Have we written about napalm or escalation to our newspaper, our congressman or the Pentagon? Perhaps we believe it's hopeless, but we'd do better to believe in the sacramental order. Grace always comes wrapped in a sensible sign—maybe a book we lend, a phone call, a letter mailed today, an encouraging remark or some trouble we put ourselves to for the sake of others.

To pray is to let God into our life so that he'll help us let our neighbor in as well. Pharisees are guilty on two counts: they receive nothing from God and give nothing to others. Never having experienced his mercy, they feel no pity for their fellow sinners; never having loved him, they can't love anyone else.

God doesn't want adorers; he wants co-workers. An adoring husband or wife may flatter us at first, but in the long run there's nothing more tedious. The best spouse is a co-worker. Naturally, there'll be moments of closeness and contemplation, when we tell one another how we enjoy working together; but if we're forever talking about our joy, our work doesn't get done. Believe me, there's nothing more detrimental in Christianity than a certain idea of contemplation.

Saint John reminds us twice that "no one has

ever seen God."[3] Granted that the Son has revealed
him to us—"whoever sees me, sees the one who sent
me"[4]—still the only God we can contemplate is the incarnate God: God the Savior, God the Redeemer, the
God who gives himself unreservedly, the God who lays
down his life—in a word, the God who serves us. How
can we contemplate him sincerely, then, and not be
moved to do like him? How contemplate a God who
works perpetually—"My Father goes on working, and
so do I"[5]—and remain mere onlookers?

Let's pursue this matter still further. There are
two ways of looking at prayer; and, even among the
knowledgeable, there's a whole vocabulary that should
be changed. (A man can sanctify himself in spite of
misconceptions, but it's wiser to give him accurate
words and ideas to function with.) Some of us foolishly
argue, "We should be glad to waste time in God's presence, glad to squander it on him alone!" But God
doesn't want anything just for himself, because he's
never alone and never egoistic. All he thinks of is saving the world, not monopolizing our time. We may as
well say, "I'm going to baby-sit with the Child Jesus,
keep him company and please him by staying there and
frittering away my time with him. I'll take care of him,
incense him, love and serve him." If that's how we in-
terpret the motto "God first must be loved and served,"
we haven't grasped a single thing.

[3] 1 Jn. 4, 12.
[4] Jn. 12, 45.
[5] Jn. 5, 17.

Look at the Gospel. On every page, we see Christ serving us. He has us sit down, waits on us and offers us his bread; he pacifies and relaxes us, puts us at ease and makes us happy; he washes our feet with love and reverence though we don't reverence or love ourselves. We should let him continue doing that for us in prayer, for hours on end and as often and long as possible. But once he has done it and we've understood, we'll know one thing for certain: we have to go out and do the same for others.

"What about God-centeredness?" some will ask. "Isn't everything in our life supposed to be directed toward God?" Yes, indeed, but we usually think God-centeredness means consecrating ourselves to the worship of God, whereas it means doing what he wants to do in our hearts. When he gives us his bread, he hopes we'll learn to give ours; when he washes our feet, he hopes we'll learn to shine one another's shoes. He has only one desire; and if we fulfill it, our whole life—not just the time we spend in church—becomes God-centered. Provided we recognize him in our brothers and love them with his love, we belong wholly to him.

God isn't the object of our worship and love so much as the motive power behind them. His grace is what makes us love. So we must allow him to do in us what he yearns to do: love and serve—not himself, but others. We must become meek and humble of heart like him. It will turn our life topsy-turvy, but we'll soon discover that, for once, everything is in its right place, its true place.

To sum up this second point, what does praying for others really consist in? It consists in letting ourselves be filled with God's love for them—with an active love that sacrifices its life, a sacramental love that always expresses itself outwardly. Love is essentially communicative and uniquely communicable. It influences others directly, immediately. When we love someone, we can be sure he senses it right away, almost as if on airwaves; if he's the least bit perceptive, he knows it even with his eyes closed, he feels our gaze and turns toward us. There's more communication between people than we suspect, but it takes place only if our love is genuine—that is, active. Love that's full of excuses isn't love at all. "I'll pray for you" doesn't dispense us from exertion; on the contrary, it should mean "I'll fill my heart with so much love that I'll be ready to do anything for you." Once prayer has brought us to that pitch, our love instantly becomes efficacious. In other words, it's miraculously energetic only because it's true love and because we're truly determined to move mountains.

In conclusion, a word about suffering. Offering our pain is exactly like offering our prayers: they're both useless. Only love is communicable; only love is active. Suffering isn't active, and let's hope it isn't communicable.

For that reason, we should concentrate on love, not pain. Suffering is the last thing to offer up, because it's an evil. If it were precious, we'd have to cultivate, extend and intensify it. Unfortunately, some Christians do: they make pilgrimages barefooted, put cinders in their shoes and jab themselves with pins in an effort to please God, as if he were some kind of Moloch who demands blood and smoke. Pain isn't a fit offering, since it has no value. Otherwise, Christ would have exhorted us, "Suffer and make one another suffer." (We do, but without divine ordinance.)

I emphasize this point because I work in hospitals a great deal and have come to realize that there's nothing more disheartening to a sick person in this day and age than to be told, "Offer up your pain, capitalize on it." To them, this is like saying, "You're just a wreck and can't do anything else; so now that you're on your last legs, make the most of your suffering anyway." How thoughtless! What the sick need to hear now is something like this: "You're as much of a man as anybody else. We're all more or less sick, more or less dotty these days. You just happen to be a bit worse than the rest of us; but, sick as you are, you're still in contact with your fellow men. Tell me, do you love them? The one thing you should strive to do in the world is love others. And you—why, you can love them with a special love that you've had to dredge up from the depths of your being. For suffering can do you one great service: make it impossible for you to be satisfied with a superficial love, an inconstant love, and force you to dig down into your heart till you find a love that has more value, more meaning and more impact than any other on earth. Even if you're cut off from practically everyone, there's still your doctor and your nurse. Convert them; save the world. You can do it like anybody else."

I've heard paralytics, dragging themselves around on stumps, tell others, "Come on, we've got to do something!" And I've seen thirty-year-olders who had never stirred because they and their whole family were ashamed, suddenly come out of their shell after somebody said, "The others need you. You're as good as anyone else." All at once, they became men. Concentration on offering up their mere pain had dehumanized them; their self-pitying, alibi-minded prayer had kept them from seeing that they, too, could achieve something.

Again and again, Saint Thomas states that evil —and, therefore, suffering—is negative. We can't offer up an evil. Jesus continually fought it with cures and miracles. We mustn't present evil to God. Rather than "Offer your suffering," we should suggest, "Offer your love, for love alone has positive value. What you can give isn't your suffering, but a love that has been deepened and strengthened by it." Even in extreme cases, we're never sure that a sick person has nothing left but to offer his misery; in fact, we all know of bedridden patients who endure agony and yet bear witness, act and inspire others to act also. Is there a time in life to be doers and another to be only offerers? No, for even the most active have afflictions to bear and the most infirm possess unsuspected potential.

Instead of our prayers and sufferings, then, we must offer love. True love will impel us to act, send us out, like Christ, to save the world. But to make sure we approach the world with nothing less than his love, his dedication, his understanding and his humility, let's all go to adoration first.